THE CLASSIC DOUG DILLARD SONGBOOK OF 5 STRING BANJO TABLATURES

Song Coordination and Concept:
Lynne Robin Green, Lansdowne & Winston Music

~

New annotations created by Bill Knopf

~

Front cover photo by Will Richardson

~

With special thanks to Michael Lawson
Of Mixbooks and Artistpro.com

~

Music tablature and notation on
"What's That" and "G string Boogie" by Mark Switzer

ISBN 978-1-5724-106-8
SAN 683-8022

Contents

~ Foreword ~

I would like to thank all of my loyal fans and fellow banjo players of the world for the wonderful support you have given me throughout the years. By your own special request, here's our 'long awaited tablature book featuring my own style of playing the 5 string banjo'.

If you are an avid banjo player and want to learn how to play these tunes, this tablature is written exactly the way that I play it.

Some of these great songs are from the Andy Griffith Shows - where I played and co-starred as the Darling Family, and also from many great years of our recording's as the original Dillards, my Doug Dillard Solo Banjo albums and from The Doug Dillard Band albums, too . . . . .

Thanks again, and I hope this book will be an inspiration to all who truly love the art of playing five string banjo.

Douglas Flint Dillard from the Past to the Present
~Biography by Lynne Robin Green~

Douglas and *Rodney (The two brother's Dillard)* made their debut as part of their own family band. The family band played for square dances and pie suppers in Salem, Missouri. Their dad *Homer Sr.* played fiddle, mom *Lorene* played guitar and the oldest brother *Earl* played keyboards. They played all of the traditional songs like "Sally Goodin" and "Bill Cheatam". *Douglas Dillard*, the second of three son's was born March 6, 1937 in Salem, Missouri. As a kid he and his life long buddy Bill Glenn played up and down the streets of Salem for anyone and everyone who would listen. **Doug** originally started playing guitar at age (5) and he picked up his first banjo *(that was given to him by his parents as a Christmas present)* at the age of (15). *In 1956 Douglas played banjo on the local weekly radio show of Howe Teague at KSMO in Salem.*

From 1956 to 1959 *Doug and his younger brother Rodney along with Bill Glenn, Henry and Jim Lewis and Paul Breidenbach formed The Ozark Mountain Boys. Mitch Jayne* who was a local radio personality *(and a member of The Dillard's to come)* invited the band to play on ' *Hickory Hollow' his Saturday morning radio show on KSMO in Salem.* Doug also played banjo for *The Hawthorn Brothers* and during that time he appeared with the group " *Lee Mace and The Ozark Opry* ". *Doug learned his own very unique style of THREE-FINGER PICKING by listening to the early recordings of Earl Scrugg's , Don Reno and Ralph Stanley .* **Doug** recall's the first time he heard the music of Earl Scrugg's..." *I was driving down the road with the radio on. All of a sudden I heard this incredible banjo music. I got so excited that I drove off the road and down into a ditch. I had to be towed out. That was the beginning of one the longest lasting admiration society's in music (which is what Doug has always had for Earl Scrugg's). Young Doug wrote Earl a personal letter inquiring 'is sixteen was too young to learn the banjo? '.... Earl graciously replied and he supplied the needed encouragement. Doug then pestered his parents into driving him to Scrugg's home in Madison, Tennessee, some five hundred miles away from Salem. With courage not usually found at this young age Doug, boldly walked up to Scrugg's front door and he rang the bell. He introduced himself and asked Earl to install the Scrugg's tuners on his banjo. Earl kindly installed them and even brought out his own banjo for Doug to inspect. Earl Scrugg's WAS and will always be a great inspiration to Douglas.* Earl Scrugg's remains a motivating and inspirational force for all students of the banjo everywhere.

In 1958, **Doug and Rodney** joined up with Joel Noel and *The Dixie Ramblers.* Based in St Louis *this band featured John Hartford, Buddy Van Hoosier, and Joel Noel. (A few years later John Hartford wrote 'Gentle On My Mind' which was recorded by hundreds of musical artist's). (Douglas played banjo on the original Glen Campbell hit record of the song).* Shortly after joining The Dixie Ramblers, *Doug and Rodney began recording for Marlo Records (K-Ark Records) a St. Louis based record label. Their first single was "Banjo in The Hollow /You're On My Mind" followed by three more singles "Doug's Breakdown /My Only True Love", " Highway Of Sorrow/Mama Don't Allow", and "I Saw The Light/Cabin in Gloryland".* Soon thereafter billed as The Dillard Brother's, Doug and Rodney began to perform on their own. Doug and Rodney came to meet **Dean Webb** through Dale Sledd. (At that time Dale was in The Ozark Opry and later he joined The Osborne Brother's). *Dean Webb, a mandolin player from Independence, Missouri* was an asset to Doug and Rodney's music as he had great musical skills and pure intuitive feel for the style of music they were playing. Next came *Mitch Jayne a radio announcer at KSMO in Salem* who had been friends with Doug and Rodney for a few years. *With the help of Doug, Rodney and Dean, Mitch soon learned to play the bass fiddle. Mitch had a very keen wit filled with extremely original back home Ozark humor and a sense of natural comedic timing which combined with his bass playing rounded out the sound, look and unique personality of The Dillard's. In 1962 they played their first debut show at Washington University in St. Louis which was captured and preserved for bluegrass history (throughout the past 35 years) (remastered by Rodney Dillard) and released finally in 1999 on the album entitled DILLARDS LIVE -A LONG TIME AGO (varese). That night's first performance as The Dillards held such high energy that the crowd roared and stomped with enthusiasm over the sheer passion of the playing and singing that the Dillards group brought to the stage. Bluegrass music had finally arrived on the college campus.* The Dillards knew then that they must go to Hollywood and bring their special sound to the music world at large. So they left Salem Missouri in pursuit of a recording career in the big city. At that time most of the country music was produced in Nashville. Country music and bluegrass music was pretty much nonexistent in Hollywood. But once they arrived in Hollywood they found out about *a burgeoning folk scene that was happening at a club called The Ash Grove (which had afterhours jam session nights).* Appearing that night was *The Greenbriar Boys* (a NY based bluegrass band). *The Dillards took their instruments up onto the stage after closing time and just like in a dream the perfect opportunity opened up - as Jim Dickson an A&R man from Elektra Records happened to be there and witness this incredibly talented new group fresh* *from the Ozark's. By the next night they were quickly signed to a multi-album recording contract with Elektra Records. Dickson, who later produced the Byrds, was impressed by the novel sound of the Dillards. Dean Webb, by the way had arranged the vocal harmonies on Mr. Tambourine Man for The Byrds. The Dillards debut album for Elektra was called 'Back Porch Bluegrass'* as many of the songs had been composed on the back porch of Mitch's home in Salem. *Their next album was (" Dillards Live...Almost "),* recorded at a three night engagement at the Mecca nightclub in Los Angeles. *Around this same time, Richard Linke the Associate Producer of The Andy Griffith Show contacted Elektra Records and arranged to audition the band.* There was an opportunity on the Andy Griffith Show for the right group to play a musically inclined backwoods mountain family. *They were signed immediately as semi regular cast members and came to be known as " The Darlin Boys " on The Andy Griffith Show.* Whenever possible, Andy Griffith allowed and encouraged The Dillards to perform their own material on the show. *(They performed in many key episodes in the shows and helped to introduce the urban American television audience to the special brand of mountain music that The Dillards grew up with).* With their high-energy musical talent, and uniquely special delivery they brought bluegrass music and mountain culture to the American television audience.

The Dillards did many guest spots on other classic TV shows such as The Judy Garland Special, The Tennessee Ernie Ford Special and more, gathering really great reviews, and *(also creating some incredible live recordings) after playing The Newport Folk Festival (which was released later as Bluegrass Breakdown-Newport Folk)-(Vanguard Records) (at the Festival they shared the stage with Bill Monroe and a lot of other really classic bluegrass musicians).* They also performed to extremely responsive crowds at *The Monterey Folk Festival, The UCLA Folk Festival and New York's Folk Festival .The Dillards during this time toured with Elton John, Bob Dylan, Joan Baez, Carl Perkins and many others. On their tour to the UK they received The Edison Award in England for excellence in music.* Around that same time *Jim Dickson asked The Dillards to work with him on an instrumental project with Glen Campbell featured (on 12 string guitar) .The group was called The Folkswingers* and they recorded folk and bluegrass songs for two albums released on (The Folkswingers-12 String Guitar Volume 1 and Volume Two-on the World Pacific Label). They also did another special project *with Dickson and The Byrds called (Various Artists-Early LA-Archive Series-Volume Four)-which was released on Together Records.* Also around this time The Dillards did an *instrumental album for Elektra entitled (Pickin and Fiddlin with Byron Berline).* After that album The Dillards left Elektra and recorded some *singles for Capitol Records (Nobody Knows/Last Thing On My Mind). After this point, Douglas decided to part way's with the Dillards as he wanted to explore some new musical territories, so he joined up with The Byrd's for their European tour.* He was featured on their live European album *(The Byrds-The Live Byrds-Bulldog Records) with Roger Mc Guinn, Gram Parsons, Chris Hillman, and Kevin Kelley.* After the tour *Douglas and 'ex-byrd' Gene Clark* teamed up to create a completely new sound, *'a blend of back hills country and rock music '. The band at this time consisted of Bernie Leadon, Mike Clarke, Byron Berline, David Jackson, John Corneal, Don Beck and Donna Washburn.* This new country rock sound the groundbreaking band was making *was further embraced by later acts such as The Flying Burrito Brother's, Poco, The Eagle's and many many others. Doug and Gene Clark recorded (as The Dillard-Clark Expedition and as Dillard & Clark) the album's (Fantastic Expedition, and Through The Morning Through The Night, and Grass Roots -A&M Records) (Kansas City Southern-Doug Dillard & Gene Clark/Ariola-Eurodisc) and singles as (Dillard & Clark)-(Laying Down The Middle/Don't Be Cruel) and (Why Not You Baby/The Radio Song). The musical sound that Doug and Gene made together was definitely a forerunner of the big country meets rock sound to come.*

In 1968, Doug recorded *The Banjo Album - (Together Records) - which featured Byron Berline and also had an unbilled Gene Clark, John Hartford, Red Mitchell, Milt Holland, and Andy Belling. In 1973-1974 Doug cut two great solo albums with 20th Century Records, (You Don't Need A Reason to Sing, and Duelin Banjo). Doug also was performing in and scoring for commercials for 7-UP, Kentucky Fried Chicken, Chevrolet and Visa. Doug performed on the song ("Songbird") on an album with the group The Country Coalition (Bluesway Records)* of which the band members were Peggy and Dick Bradley, John Kurtz, and David Jackson. *Doug was a regular cast member on ' Music Country USA' (Dean Martin's summer replacement show on which he performed the Theme Song -" Music Country"). He was also seen in recurrent guest spots on The Dean Martin Show. In the late 1970's John Hartford would do a few albums in Nashville with Douglas and Rodney called 'Dillard-Hartford-Dillard', and also 'Glittergrass Hollywood Strings/Permanent Wave' for (Flying Fish Records).*

In 1976 *Doug recorded a single produced by Harry Nilsson for Warner Bros Records called ("Goin Down/Poor Old Slave"). In 1979 Douglas recorded as a solo artist for Flying Fish Records and released two very classic stellar banjo albums, "Jackrabbit" and "Heaven". Also on Flying Fish Records in the mid 1980's Doug formed " The Doug Dillard Band" with Ginger Boatwright on vocals, Roger Rasnake, David Grier and*

Jonathan Yudkin, and they recorded and released "Heartbreak Hotel" -Produced by Rodney Dillard. This album was (nominated for the Folk-Bluegrass Grammy Award in 1988). The Doug Dillard Band also recorded and released the album "What's that" (featuring guests such as David Grisman, Vassar Clements, Rodney Dillard, Mark Howard, Joe Osborne, Buddy Spicher, and John Probst). This album was later compiled with Heartbreak Hotel as a single CD set. It's interesting to note that Douglas and Rodney can be seen briefly in the Bette Midler movie 'The Rose,' playing musicians in Harry Dean Stanton's Band. The Original Dillards appear together in the video documentary -A Night In The Ozarks (produced by John Mc Euen). The Dillards also have performed onstage with many great artists such as Vince Gill, Ricky Skaggs, Earl Scruggs, and on many television shows such as Austin City Limits, Nashville Now, Grand Old Opry, and TV Specials and talk shows including Don Kirshners Rock Concert.

Douglas Dillard's extremely extensive session work includes albums with Hoyt Axton, Johnny Cash, Arlo Guthrie, Vassar Clements, Harry Nilsson, Bob Lind, Linda Ronstadt, Kay Starr, John Hartford, Glen Campbell, The Monkees, Aztec Two Step, Gene Clark, The Gosden Brothers, The Byrds, Judie Sill, Jess Pearson, James Lee Stanley, Steven Fromholz, Tom Pacheco, Michael Melford, Paul Hann, Michael Martin Murphey, Ray Park, John Anderson, Larry Groce, Michael Nesmith, Ron & Gail Davies, Jim Ringer, Millennium, Hayseed, Larry Perkins, Byron Berline, and The Beach Boys. He was also featured on (Ginger Boatwright's album-Fertile Ground/Flying Fish).

Douglas has worked on countless motion picture's both scoring and performing in Bonnie & Clyde, Junior Bonner, Vanishing Point- (Soundtrack-Vanishing Point-London Records), J.W. Coop, The Honker's, Bunny O' Hare (with Betty Davis), Robert Altman's Popeye (which he played banjo and also performed in) and the list goes on. Doug's Song's - Banjo In The Hollow and Doug's Tune are featured in the movie ' Return To Mayberry' as well as many other's that can be heard in The Original Andy Griffith Show episodes.

Doug's songs also appear on many albums such as: Back Porch Bluegrass, Dillards Live Almost, Dillards-First Time Live, Dillards-Country Tracks, Pickin and Fiddlin, Anthology-There Is A Time, Homecoming and Family Reunion, Byrd Part's, American Dreamer/Flying High, No Other (Gene Clark), Country Gazette, Hatchie Bottom Boys, Hickory Hill, Alan Munde, New Liberty, Molasses Creek, Dillard-Hartford-Dillard.

In 1998 the original Dillards performed together with Byron Berline at The Oklahoma International Bluegrass Festival, they also toured England and did a TV Special Concert for The BBC network.

"Douglas Dillard" has been inducted into The Preservation Hall Of Fame
for - (SPBGMA) -The Society for the Preservation of Bluegrass Music Of America.

Douglas Dillard received a Gibson Banjo endorsement in 1989 and was presented with a Gold Plated "Grenada Arch Top Banjo" - which is his personal instrument of choice.

" The Dillards had it all...great picking, cool songs, showmanship, and the best vocals in town".
- Herb Pedersen

If I've ever had any mystical experiences in my life, that was one of them. Before The Dillards even came on stage my hands started sweating and my legs started jumping. When they began playing, I don't think I breathed for another half hour ".
- John Mc Euen (After seeing The Dillards play at one of their early 1963 Los Angeles appearances)"

Then finally, The Dillards came to town - that was in 1963...Man, they were so hot! " I got to meet them and jam with them, I'll never forget it"
- Byron Berline

"Douglas Dillard resides in Nashville and remains alway's in demand as a banjo session wizard"...

Written by – Lynne Robin Green

Tunings

3 Tunings are used in the songs in this book

G tuning – g D G B D
C tuning – g C G B D
G modal tuning – g D G C D

Below are the songs arranged by tunings

G Tuning

Banjo in the Hollow, gDGBD
Blackeyed Susie, gDGBD
Cripple Creek, gDGBD
Cumberland Gap, gDGBD
Dooley, gDGBD
Doug's Tune, gDGBD
G String Boogie, gDGBD
Grandfathers Clock, gDGBD
Hickory Hollow, gDGBD
Jamboree, gDGBD
John Hardy, gDGBD
John Henry, gDGBD
Little Maggie, gDGBD
Lonesome Indian, gDGBD
Sinkin' Creek, gDGBD
Old Joe Clark, gDGBD
Old Home Place, gDGBD
What's That, gDGBD

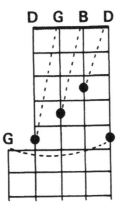

Tune you're banjo by matching the sound or pitch of an open string with a fretted note on a lower string:

1. <u>Match</u> the sound of the open third string with the sound of the fourth string fifth fret.
2. <u>Match</u> the sound of the open second string with the sound of the third string fourth fret.
3. <u>Match</u> the sound of the first string with the sound of the second string third fret.
4. <u>Match</u> the sound of the fifth string with the sound of the first string fifth fret.

C Tuning

Buckin' Mule, gCGBD
Green Corn, gCGBD

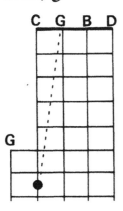

"G" tuning to "C" tuning.
Change only the fourth string.
1. Just drop or lower the sound of the fourth string "two frets". The seventh fret <u>matches</u> the open third string.

G Modal Tuning

Whole World Round, gDGCD

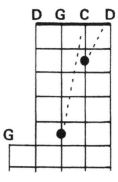

"G" tuning to "G modal" tuning.
Ghange only the second string.
1. Raise the sound or pitch of the second string up one fret so it <u>matches</u> the third string/ fifth fret.
2. You can double check by matching the sound of the second string/second fret to the sound of the open first string.

~Chords for the G Tuning~
g D G B D

Major Chords in Open Position

 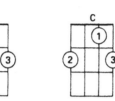 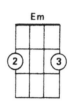

Minor Chords in Open Position

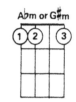 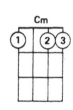

Major Chords in Closed Position

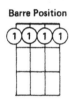

Minor Chords in Closed Position

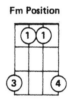 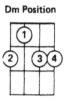

Fret No.

Fret	Major Barre		Fret	Major F		Fret	Major D	
1	G♯	A♭	1	F		1	C♯	D♭
2	A		2	F♯	G♭	2	D	
3	A♯	B♭	3	G		3	D♯	E♭
4	B		4	G♯	A♭	4	E	
5	C		5	A		5	F	
6	C♯	D♭	6	A♯	B♭	6	F♯	G♭
7	D		7	B		7	G	
8	D♯	E♭	8	C		8	G♯	A♭
9	E		9	C♯	D♭	9	A	
10	F		10	D		10	A♯	B♭
11	F♯	G♭	11	D♯	E♭	11	B	
12	G		12	E		12	C	
13	G♯	A♭	13	F		13	C♯	D♭
14	A		14	F♯	G♭	14	D	
15	A♯	B♭	15	G		15	D♯	E♭

Fret	Minor Fm		Fret	Minor Am		Fret	Minor Dm	
1	Fm		1	Am		1	C♯m	D♭m
2	F♯m	G♭m	2	A♯m	B♭m	2	Dm	
3	Gm		3	Bm		3	D♯m	E♭m
4	G♯m	A♭m	4	Cm		4	Em	
5	Am		5	C♯m	D♭m	5	Fm	
6	A♯m	B♭m	6	Dm		6	F♯m	G♭m
7	Bm		7	D♯m	E♭m	7	Gm	
8	Cm		8	Em		8	G♯m	A♭m
9	C♯m	D♭m	9	Fm		9	Am	
10	Dm		10	F♯m	G♭m	10	A♯m	B♭m
11	D♯m	E♭m	11	Gm		11	Bm	
12	Em		12	G♯m	A♭m	12	Cm	
13	Fm		13	Am		13	C♯m	D♭m
14	F♯m	G♭m	14	A♯m	B♭m	14	Dm	
15	Gm		15	Bm		15	D♯m	E♭m

Seventh Chords in Open Position

G7   D7   E7 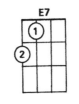   B7 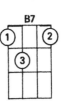   Eb7 or D#7

Seventh Chords in Closed Position

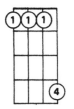

Fret No.

Fret	Chord
1	G#7 Ab7
2	A7
3	A#7 Bb7
4	B7
5	C7
6	C#7 Db7
7	D7
8	D#7 Eb7
9	E7
10	F7
11	F#7 Gb7
12	G7
13	G#7 Ab7
14	A7
15	A#7 Bb7

Fret	Chord
1	D#7 Eb7
2	E7
3	F7
4	F#7 Gb7
5	G7
6	G#7 Ab7
7	A7
8	A#7 Bb7
9	B7
10	C7
11	C#7 Db7
12	D7
13	D#7 Eb7
14	E7
15	F7

Fret	Chord
1	F7
2	F#7 Gb7
3	G7
4	G#7 Ab7
5	A7
6	A#7 Bb7
7	B7
8	C7
9	C#7 Db7
10	D7
11	D#7 Eb7
12	E7
13	F7
14	F#7 Gb7
15	G7

Fret	Chord
1	C7
2	C#7 Db7
3	D7
4	D#7 Eb7
5	E7
6	F7
7	F#7 Gb7
8	G7
9	G#7 Ab7
10	A7
11	A#7 Bb7
12	B7
13	C7
14	C#7 Db7
15	D7

Fret	Chord
1	E7
2	F7
3	F#7 Gb7
4	G7
5	G#7 Ab7
6	A7
7	A#7 Bb7
8	B7
9	C7
10	C#7 Db7
11	D7
12	D#7 Eb7
13	E7
14	F7
15	F#7 Gb7

~Chords for the C Tuning~
g C G B D

Major Chords in Open Position

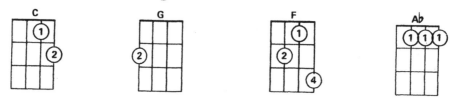

Major Chords in Closed Position

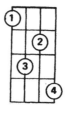

Fret No.

Fret		
1	C♯	D♭
2	D	
3	D♯	E♭
4	E	
5	F	
6	F♯	G♭
7	G	
8	G♯	A♭
9	A	
10	A♯	B♭
11	B	
12	C	
13	C♯	D♭
14	D	
15	D♯	E♭

Fret		
1	G♯	A♭
2	A	
3	A♯	B♭
4	B	
5	C	
6	C♯	D♭
7	D	
8	D♯	E♭
9	E	
10	F	
11	F♯	G♭
12	G	
13	G♯	A♭
14	A	
15	A♯	B♭

Fret		
1	F♯	G♭
2	G	
3	G♯	A♭
4	A	
5	A♯	B♭
6	B	
7	C	
8	C♯	D♭
9	D	
10	D♯	E♭
11	E	
12	F	
13	F♯	G♭
14	G	
15	G♯	A♭

Fret		
1		A
2	A♯	B♭
3	B	
4	C	
5	C♯	D♭
6	D	
7	D♯	E♭
8	E	
9	F	
10	F♯	G♭
11	G	
12	G♯	A♭
13	A	
14	A♯	B♭
15	B	

~Chords for the G Modal Tuning~
g D G C D

Major Chords in Open Position

Minor Chords in Open Position

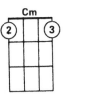

Major Chords in Closed Position

Minor Chords in Closed Position

  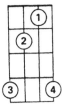

Fret No.

Fret	Note		Fret	Note		Fret	Note		Fret	Note		Fret	Note		Fret	Note	
1	C#	Db	1	A		1	F#	Gb	1	C#m	Dbm	1	A#m	Bbm	1	F#m	Gbm
2	D		2	A#	Bb	2	G		2	Dm		2	Bm		2	Gm	
3	D#	Eb	3	B		3	G#	Ab	3	D#m	Ebm	3	Cm		3	G#m	Abm
4	E		4	C		4	A		4	Em		4	C#m	Dbm	4	Am	
5	F		5	C#	Db	5	A#	Bb	5	Fm		5	Dm		5	A#m	Bbm
6	F#	Gb	6	D		6	B		6	F#m	Gbm	6	D#m	Ebm	6	Bm	
7	G		7	D#	Eb	7	C		7	Gm		7	Em		7	Cm	
8	G#	Ab	8	E		8	C#	Db	8	G#m	Abm	8	Fm		8	C#m	Dbm
9	A		9	F		9	D		9	Am		9	F#m	Gbm	9	Dm	
10	A#	Bb	10	F#	Gb	10	D#	Eb	10	A#m	Bbm	10	Gm		10	D#m	Ebm
11	B		11	G		11	E		11	Bm		11	G#m	Abm	11	Em	
12	C		12	G#	Ab	12	F		12	Cm		12	Am		12	Fm	
13	C#	Db	13	A		13	F#	Gb	13	C#m	Dbm	13	A#m	Bbm	13	F#m	Gbm
14	D		14	A#	Bb	14	G		14	Dm		14	Bm		14	Gm	
15	D#	Eb	15	B		15	G#	Ab	15	D#m	Ebm	15	Cm		15	G#m	Abm

Banjo in the Hollow

Music by:
Douglas Dillard and
Rodney Dillard

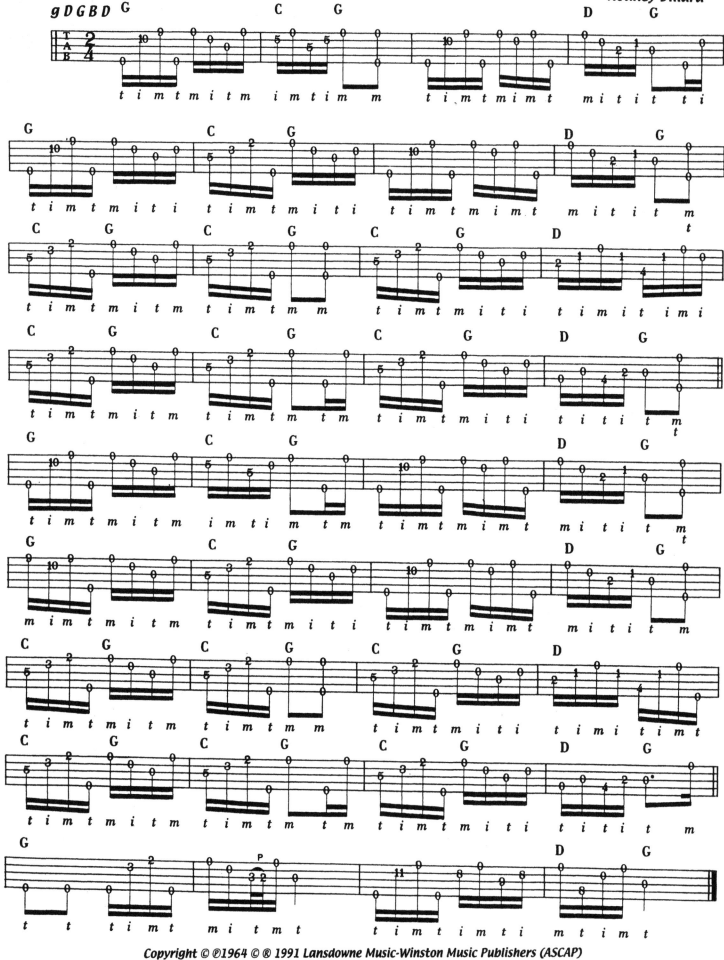

Blackeyed Susie

Traditional

Arranged by:
Douglas Dillard

Oth - er night I went to town, met a lit - tle girl named Sus - ie Brown. Her eyes were black and her hair was brown____ *Chorus* that lit - tle girl laid this man down____ Hey! Lit - tle black - eyed Sus - ie, Ho! pret - ty, black - eyed Sus - ie. Hey! Lit - tle black - eyed Sus - ie Ho! pret-ty, black - eyed Sus - ie

2. Fell in love the very same night;
   went to the preacher, treated him right.
   Tied the knot so very tight;
   promised him we would not fight.   (Chorus)

3. All I need to make me happy,
   two little boys to call me pappy;
   one named Paul, the other named Davy,
   one loves ham, the other gravy.   (Chorus)

13

Blackeyed Susie

Traditional

Arranged by:
Douglas Dillard

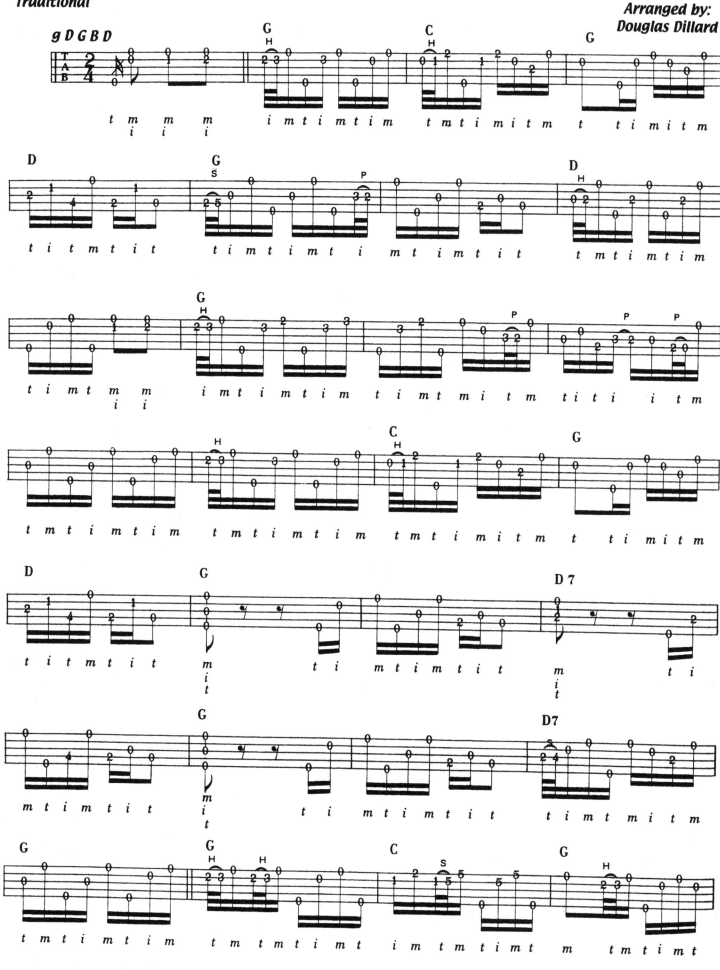

14

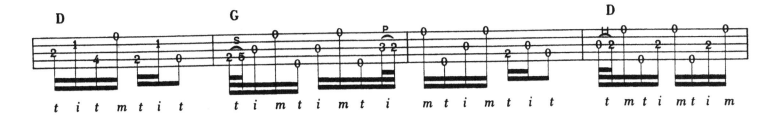

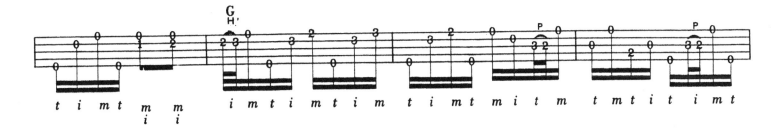

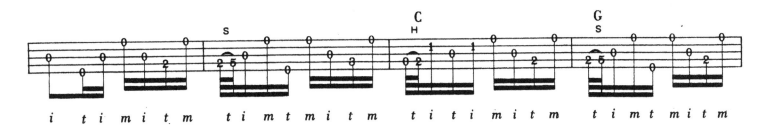

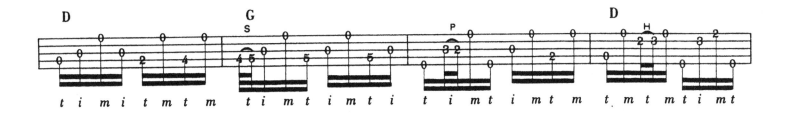

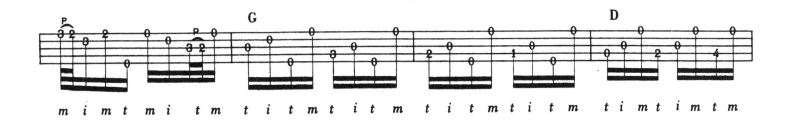

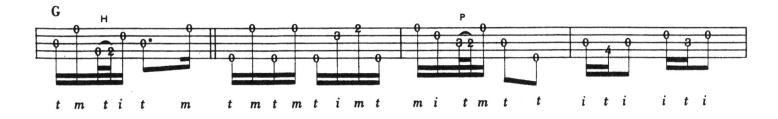

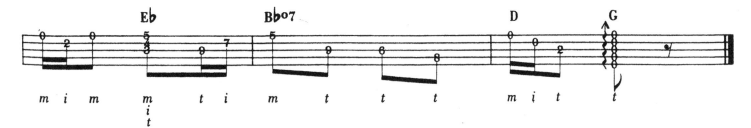

Cripple Creek

Traditional

Arrangement by:
Douglas Dillard

1. Come on John and get your pole, fish-es is bit-in' at the Crip-ple Creek Hole. Bag of crick-ets, twen-ty foot line, rock for a sink-er and a gal-lon of shine. Go-in' up Crip-ple Creek go-in' on a run, go-in' up Crip-ple Creek to have a lit-tle fun. roll my britch-es to my knees,__ wade ole Crip-ple Creek when I please.__

2. I got a girl and she loves me, she's a sweet as she can be.
   She's got eyes of baby blue, makes my gun shoot straight and true.

(To Chorus:)

Cripple Creek

Traditional

Arrangement by:
Douglas Dillard

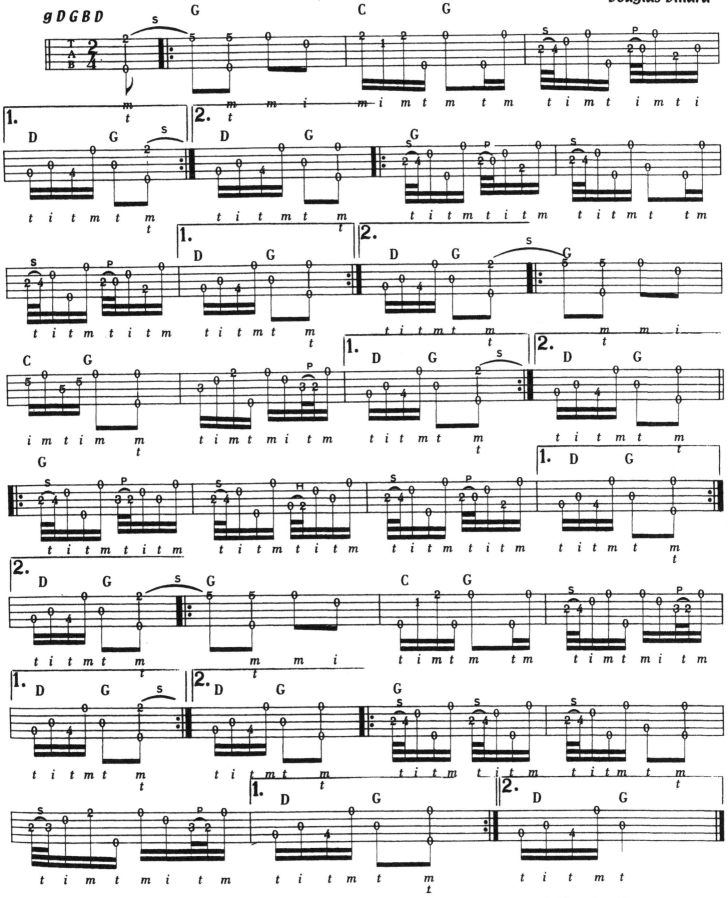

Try playing the first section of "BANJO IN THE HOLLOW" as a variation for the first section of "CRIPPLE CREEK"

Cumberland Gap

Traditional

Arranged by:
Douglas Dillard

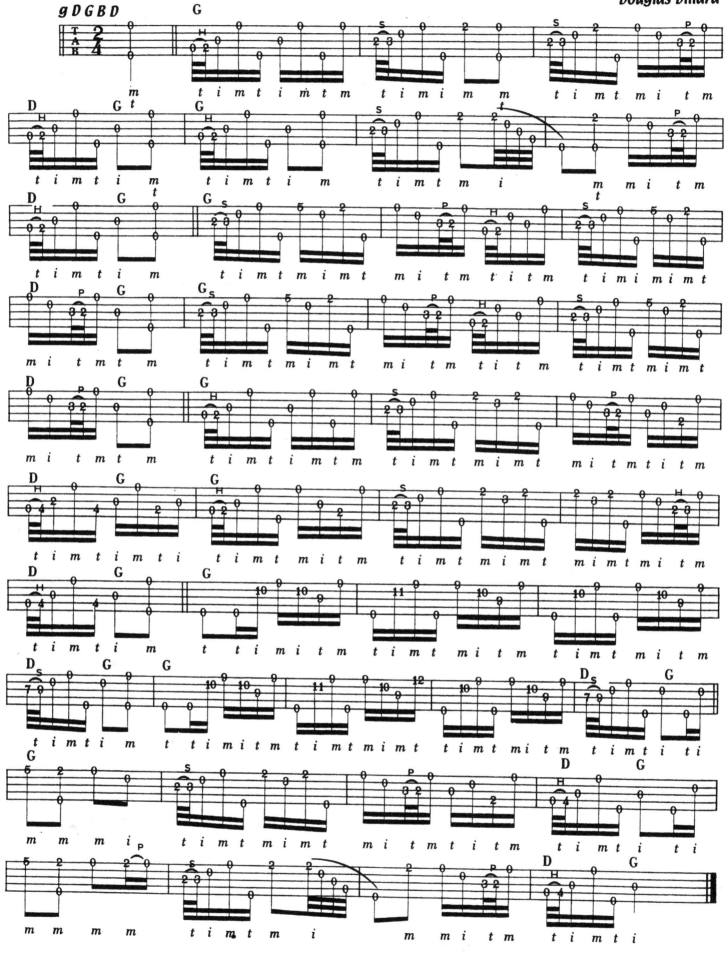

Dooley

Arranged by: Douglas Dillard
Words by: Mitch Jayne
Music by: Rodney Dillard

2. The revenuers came for him, a-slippin' thru the woods.
Dooley kept behind them all and never lost his goods.
Dooley was a trader when into town he come,
sugar by the bushel and molasses by the ton.

3. I remember very well the day old Dooley died,
the women folk looked sorry and the men stood 'round and cried.
Now Dooley's on the mountain, he lies there all alone,
they put a jug beside him and a barrel for a stone.

Dooley

Arranged by: Douglas Dillard
Words by: Mitch Jayne
Music by: Rodney Dillard

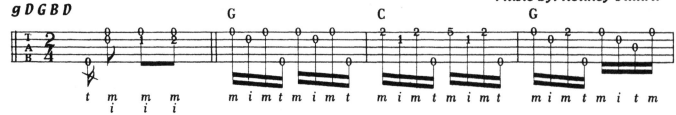

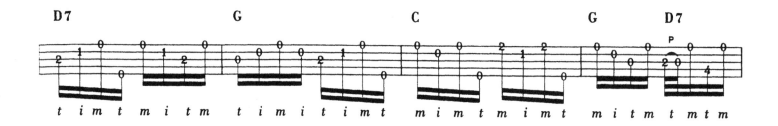

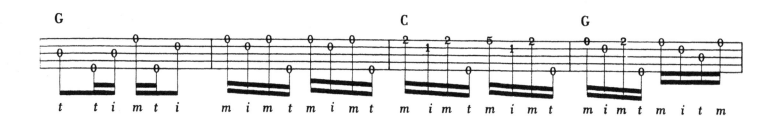

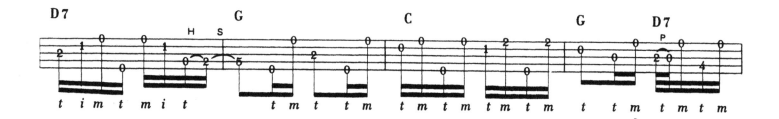

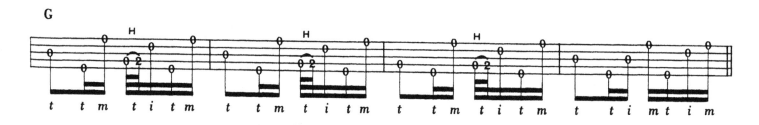

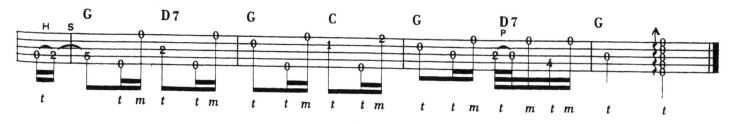

After the final chorus play this tag ending:

20

Chord Rhythm Pattern

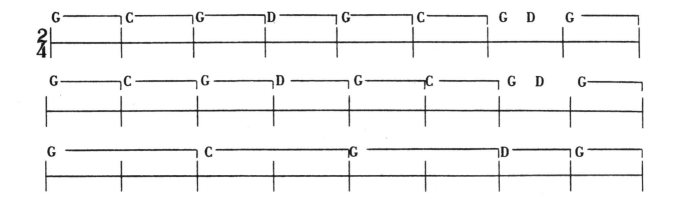

Suggested Back-up Pattern

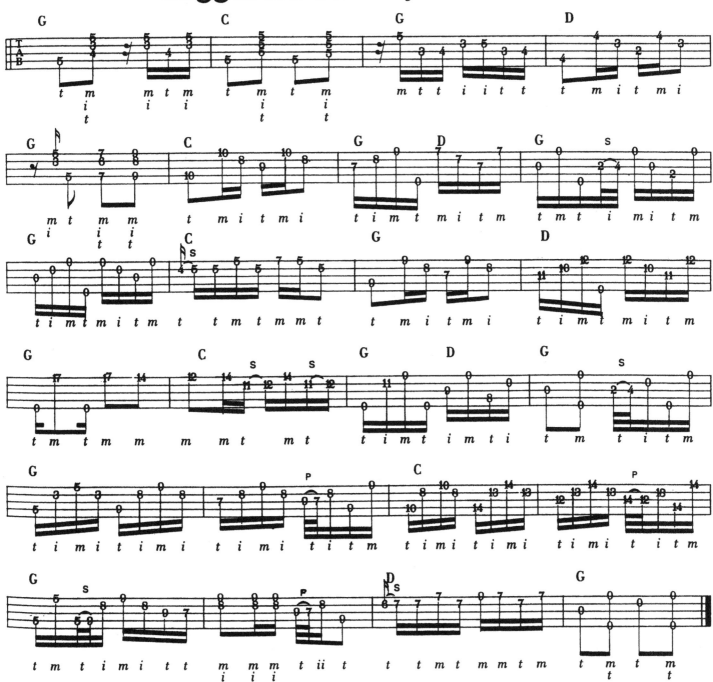

Doug's Tune
(My Grass is Blue)

Music by:
Douglas Dillard

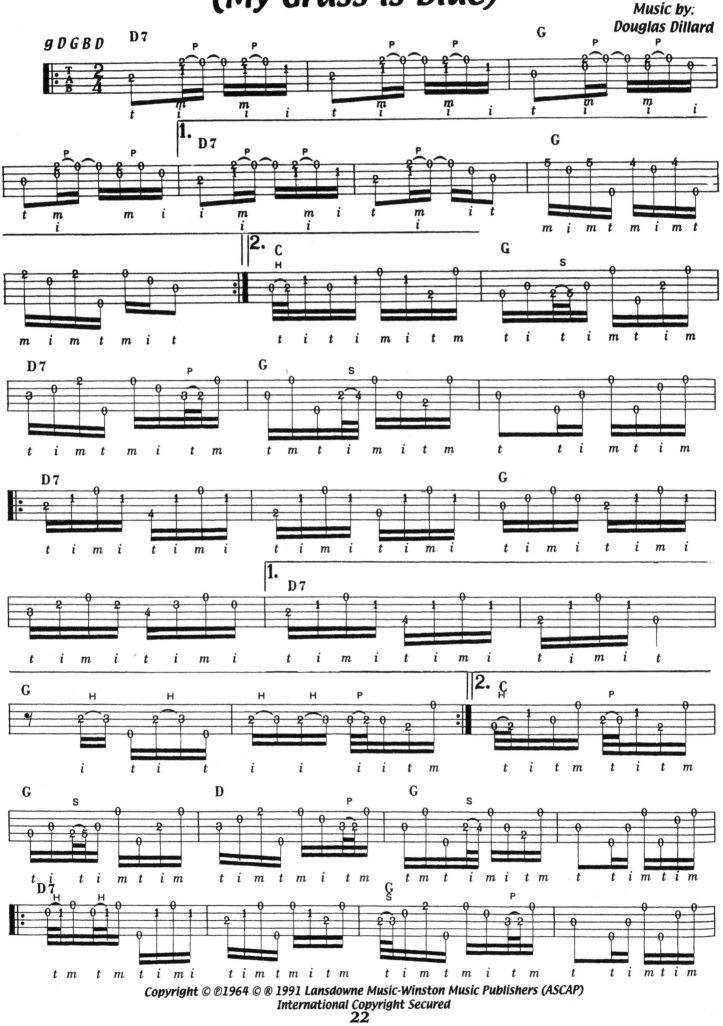

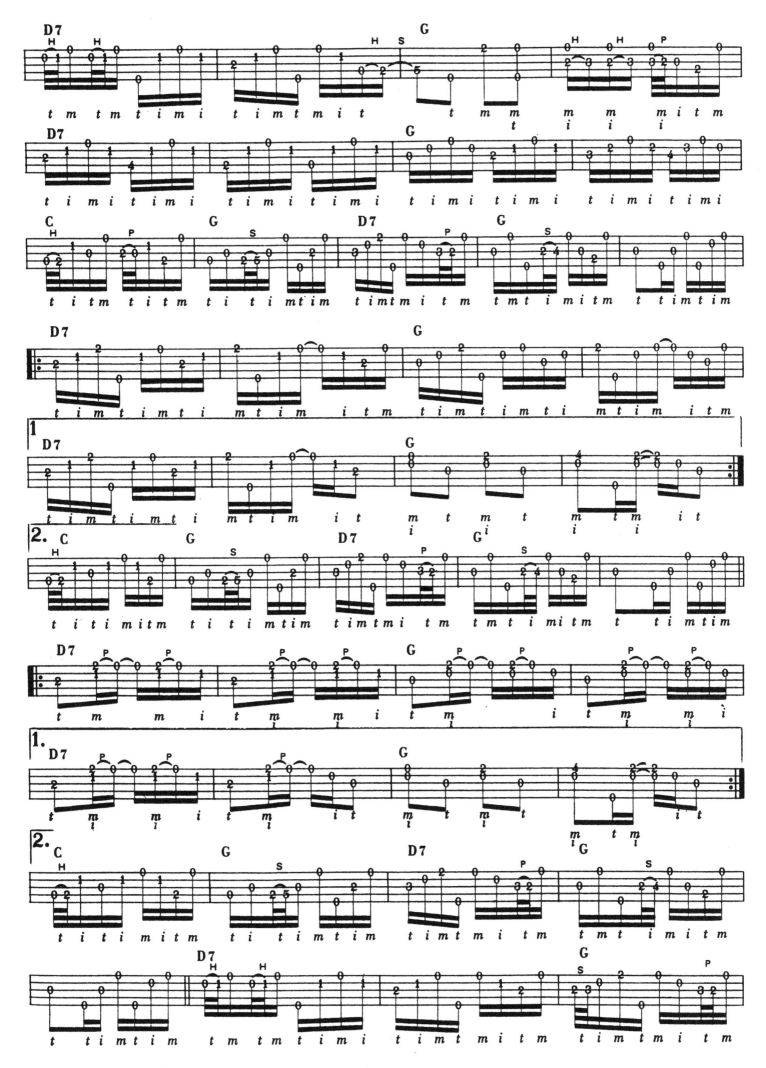

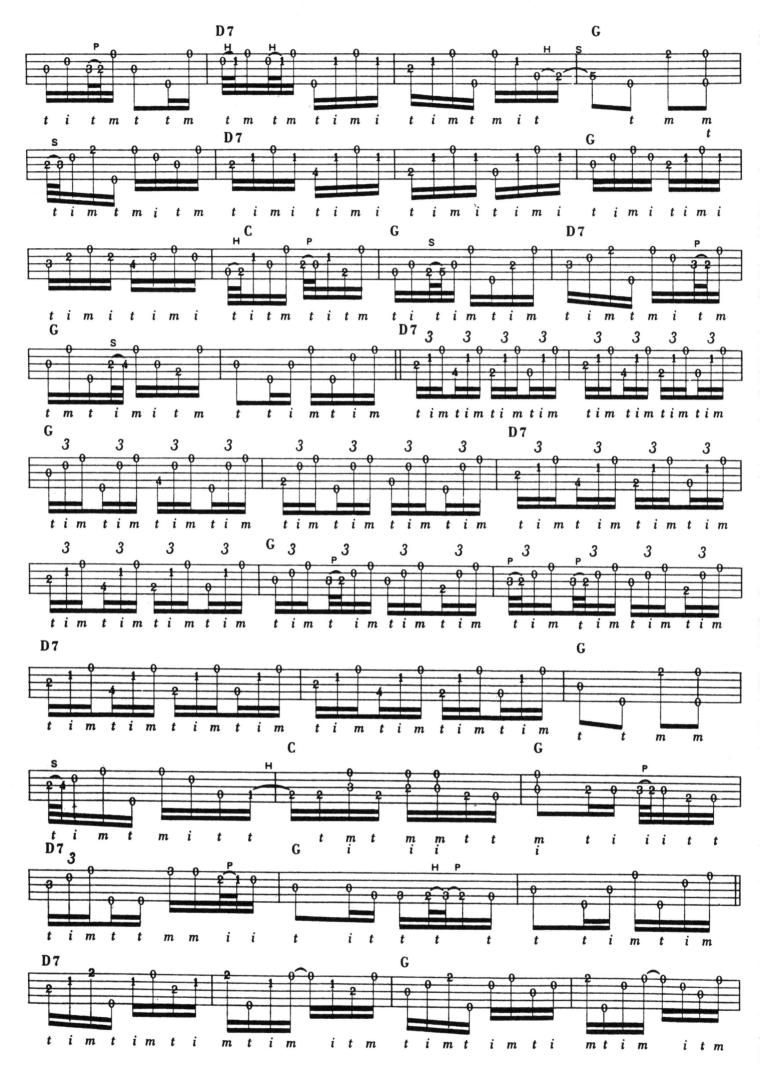

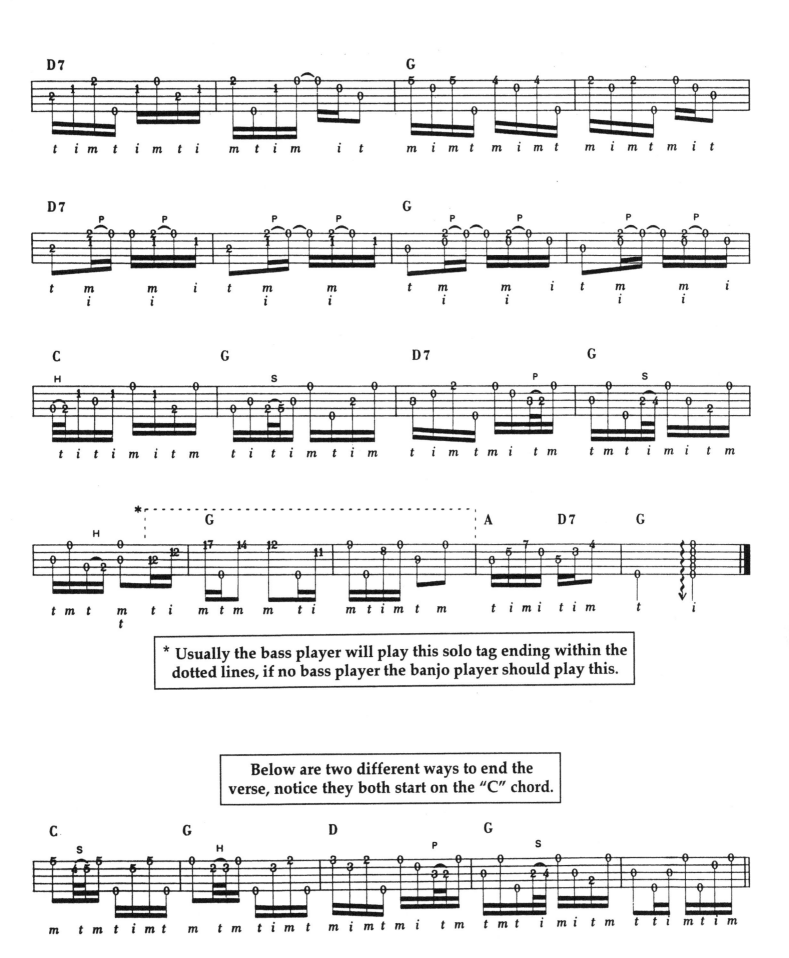

* Usually the bass player will play this solo tag ending within the dotted lines, if no bass player the banjo player should play this.

Below are two different ways to end the verse, notice they both start on the "C" chord.

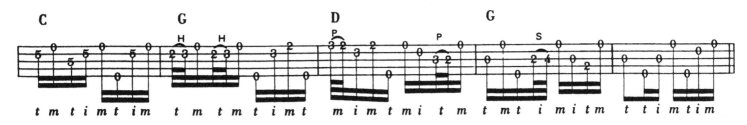

G String Boogie

Music by:
Douglas Dillard

G String Boogie

Music by:
Douglas Dillard

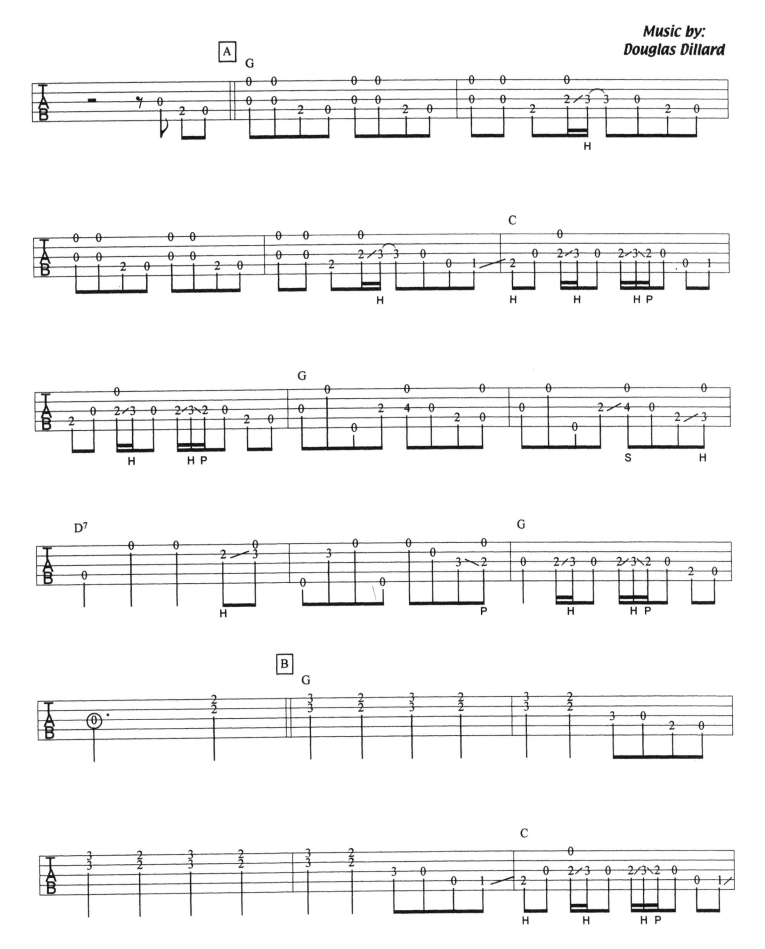

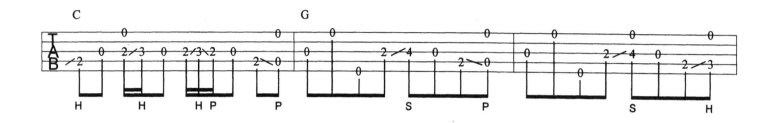

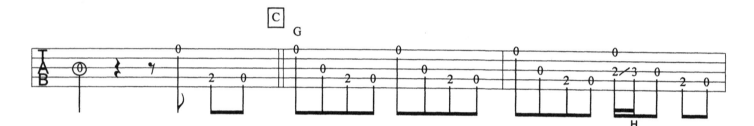

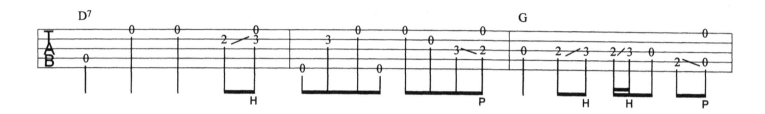

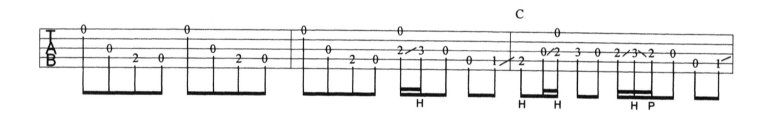

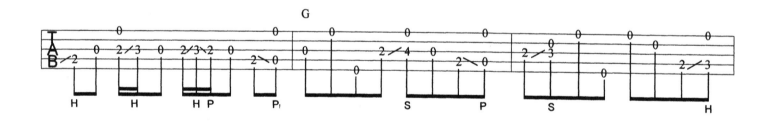

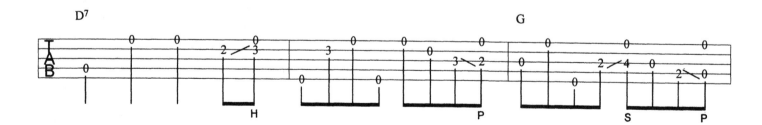

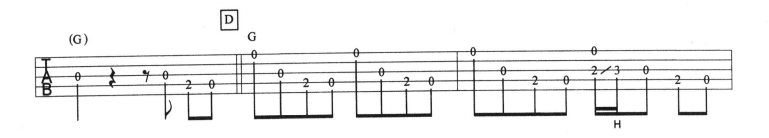

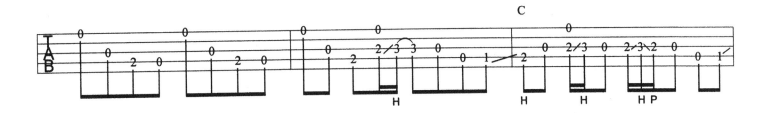

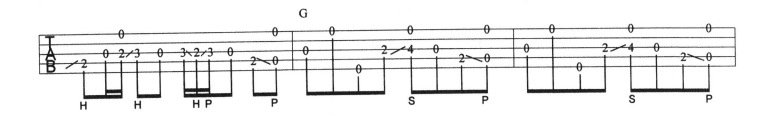

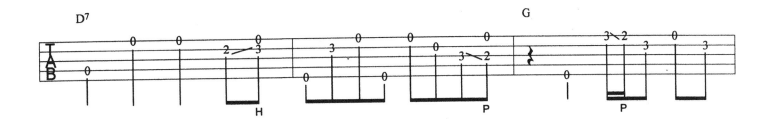

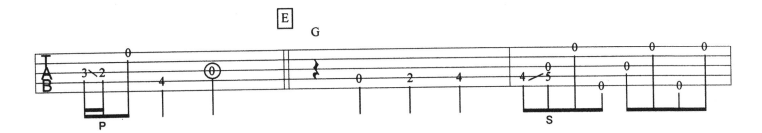

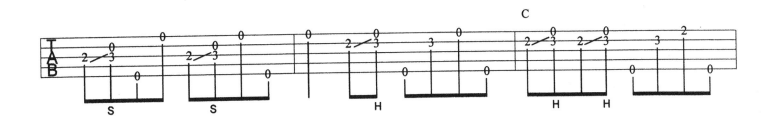

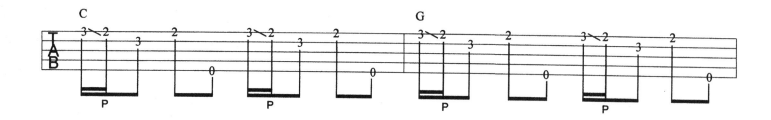

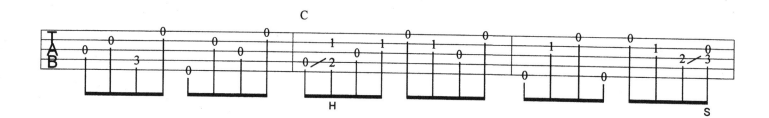

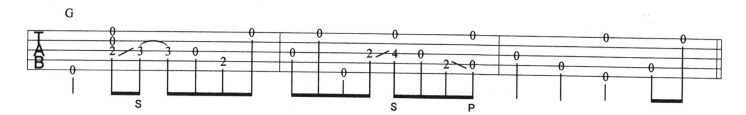

F

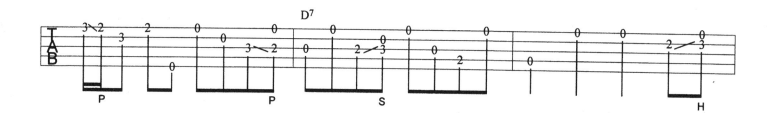

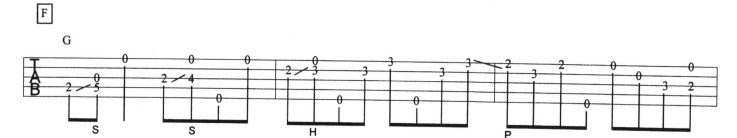

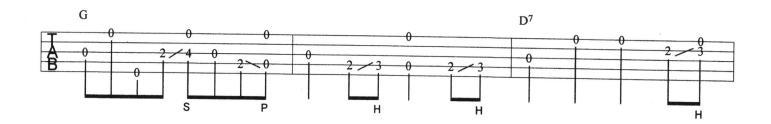

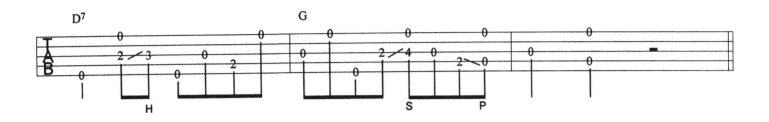

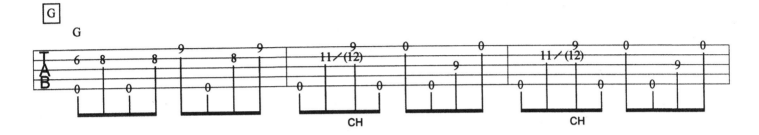

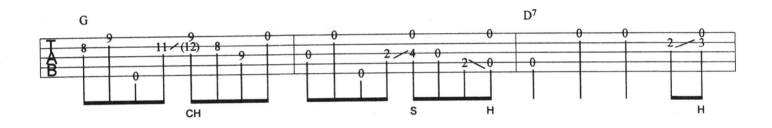

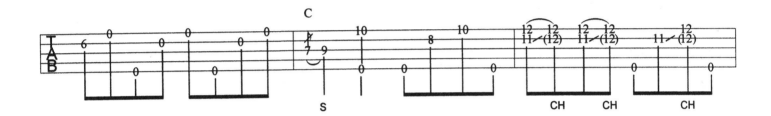

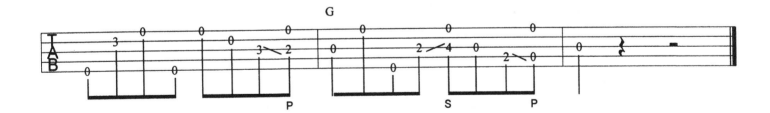

Grandfathers Clock

Traditional

Arranged by:
Douglas Dillard

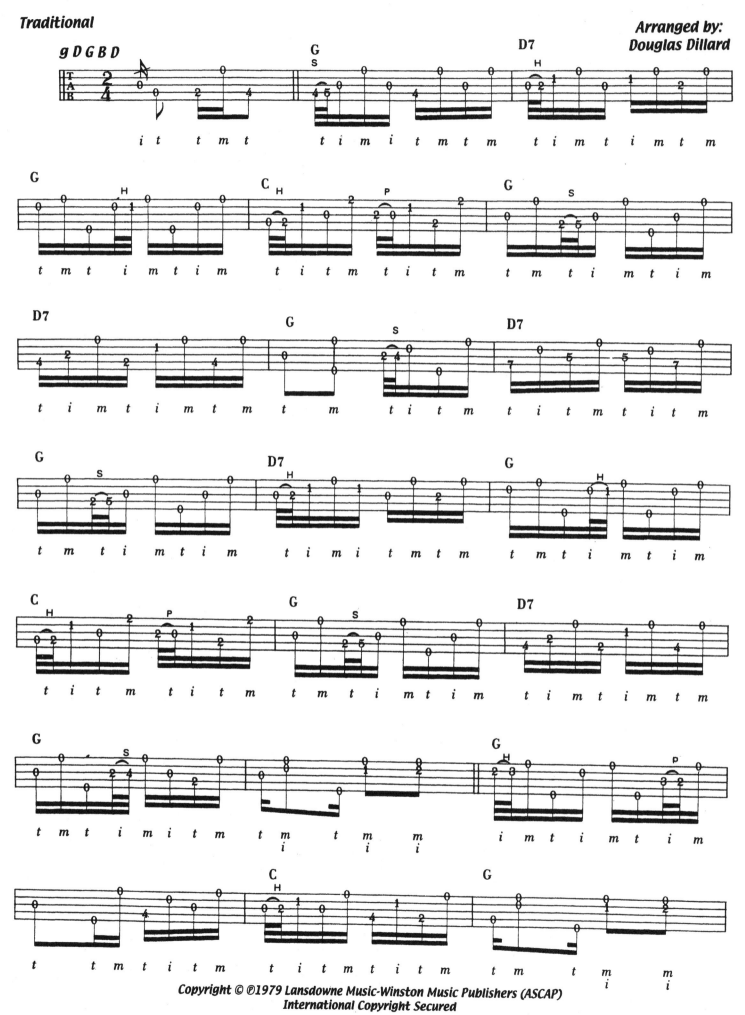

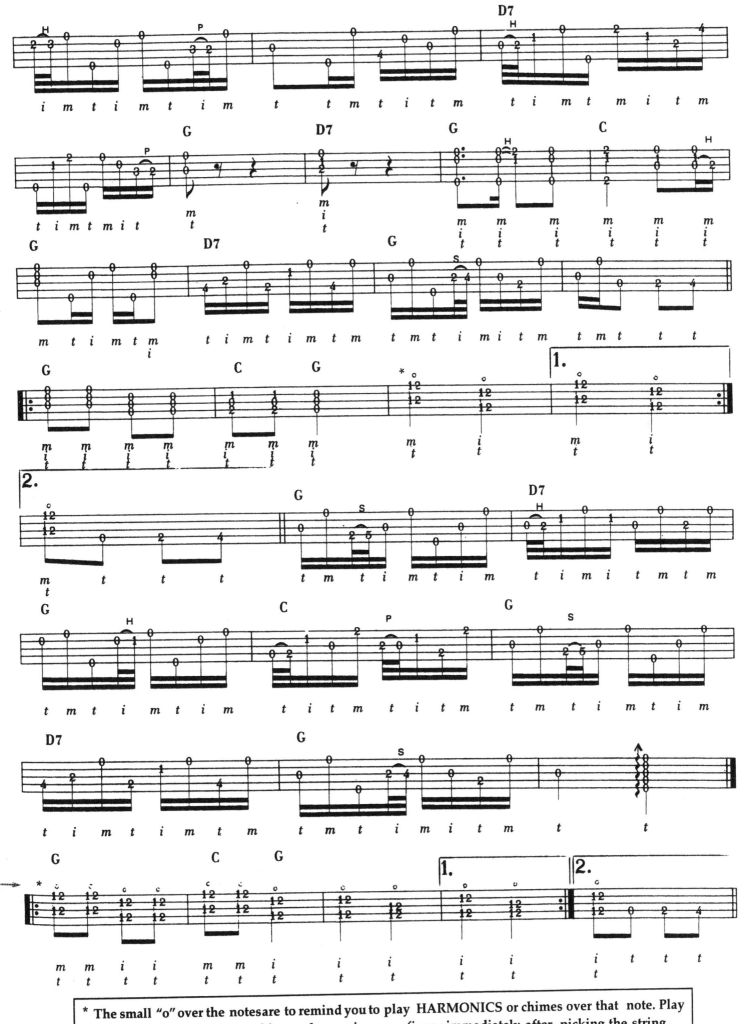

* The small "o" over the notes are to remind you to play HARMONICS or chimes over that note. Play the harmonic by lightly touching and removing your finger immediately after picking the string.

Hickory Hollow

Music by:
Douglas Dillard

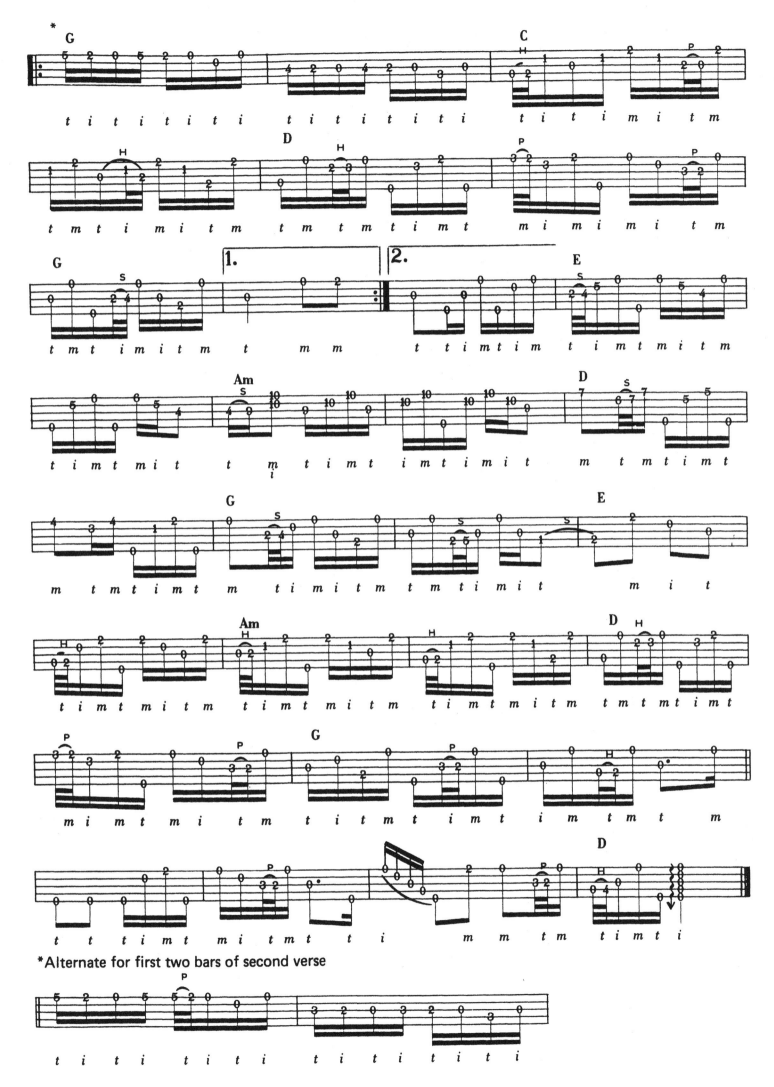

*Alternate for first two bars of second verse

35

Jamboree

Arranged by: Douglas Dillard
Music by: Andrew Belling

John Hardy

Traditional

Arranged by:
Douglas Dillard

John Hardy got to that East Stone Bridge,
he thought that he would be free.
But up stepped the sheriff and took him by the arm
sayin', "Johnny, come and walk along with me,
Johnny, come and walk along with me."

John Hardy had a pretty little girl,
the dress that she wore was blue
as she came down to that ole 'jail cell,
sayin', "Johnny, I've been true to you,
Johnny, I've been true to you.

I've been to the east and I've been to the west,
I've travelled this wild world 'round.
I've been to the river, and I've been baptized.
And now I'm on my hangin' ground.
now I'm on my hangin' ground.

John Hardy

Traditional

Arranged by:
Douglas Dillard

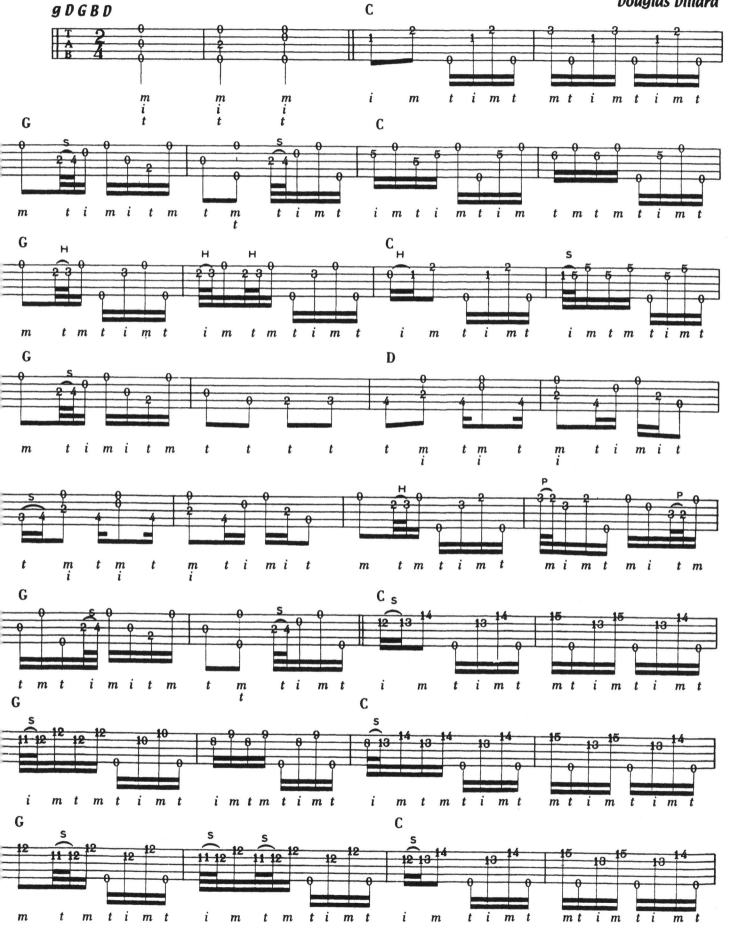

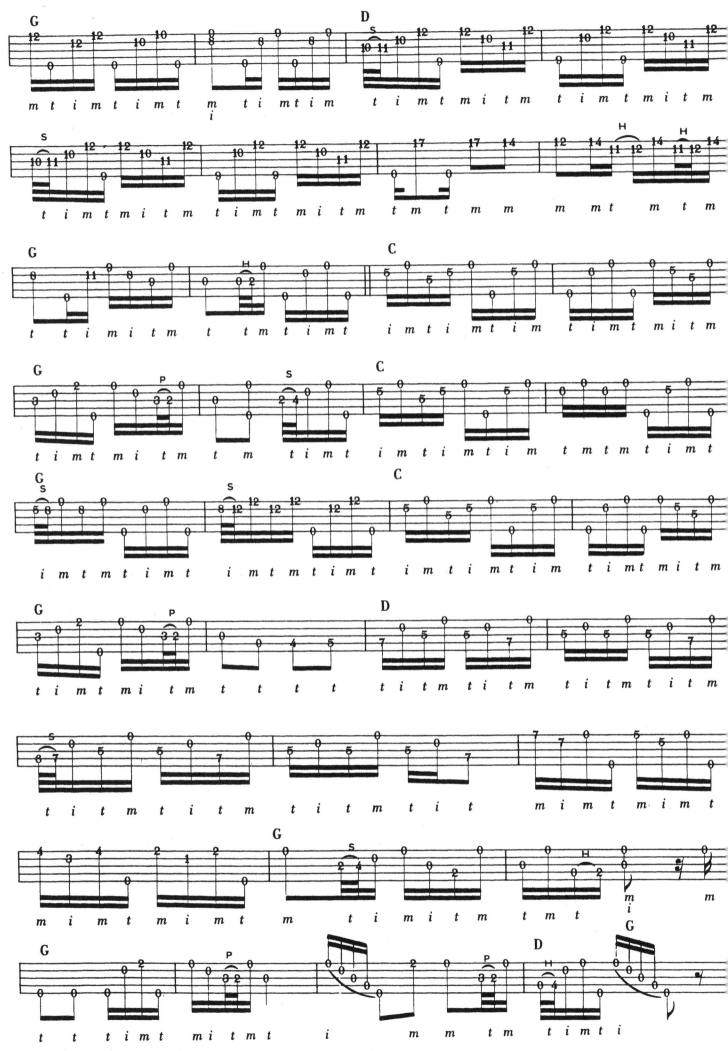

40

John Henry

Traditional

Arrangement by:
Douglas Dillard

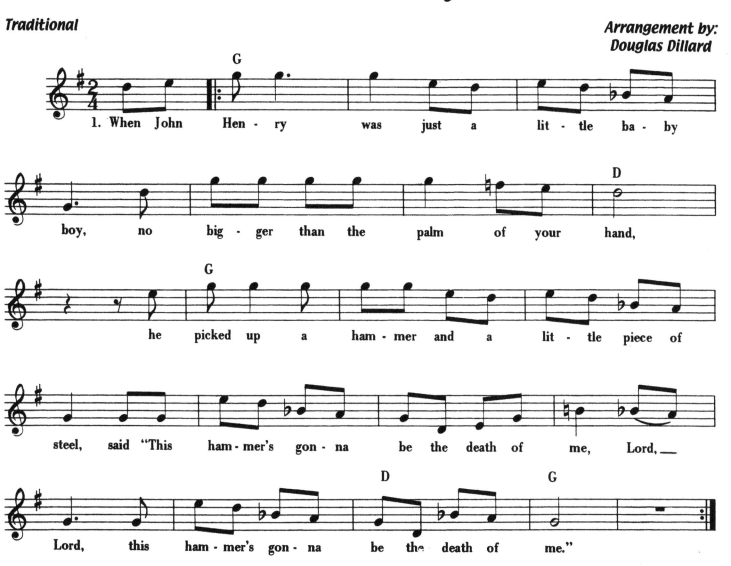

2. John Henry had a little woman,
   her name was Polly Ann.
   John Henry took sick and he had to go to bed,
   Polly drove that steel like a man, Lord, Lord,
   Polly drove that steel like a man.

3. They took John Henry to the graveyard,
   and they laid him under the sand.
   Now every locomotive comes a-rollin' 'round
   says, "Yonder lies that steel-driving man, Lord, Lord,
   yonder lies that steel-driving man.

John Henry

Traditional

Arrangement by
Douglas Dillard

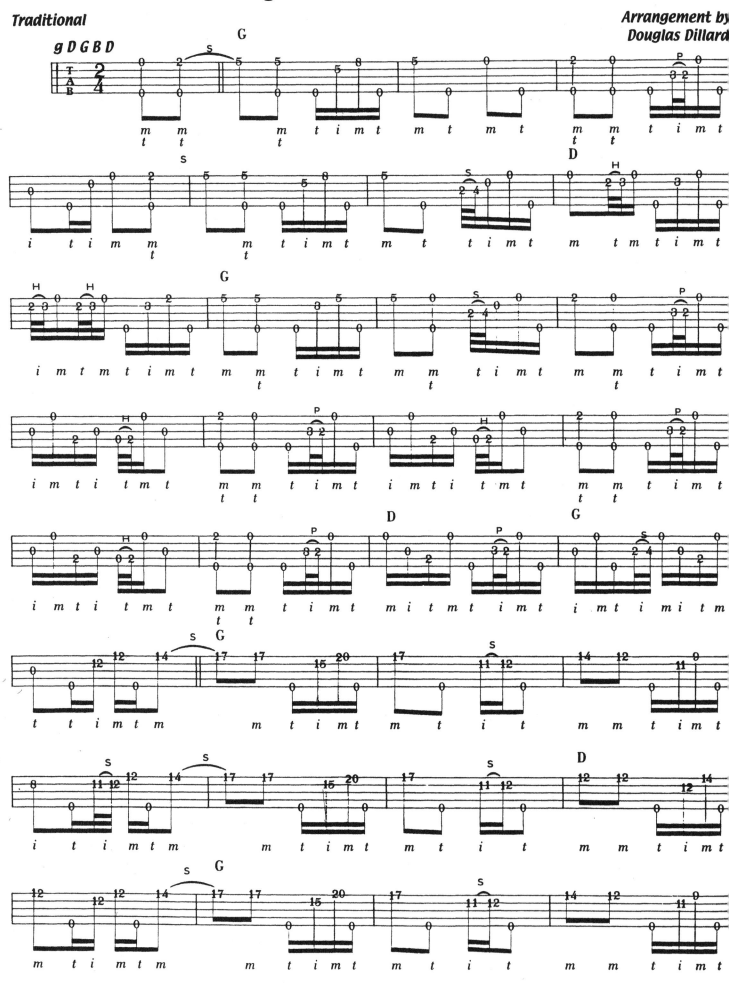

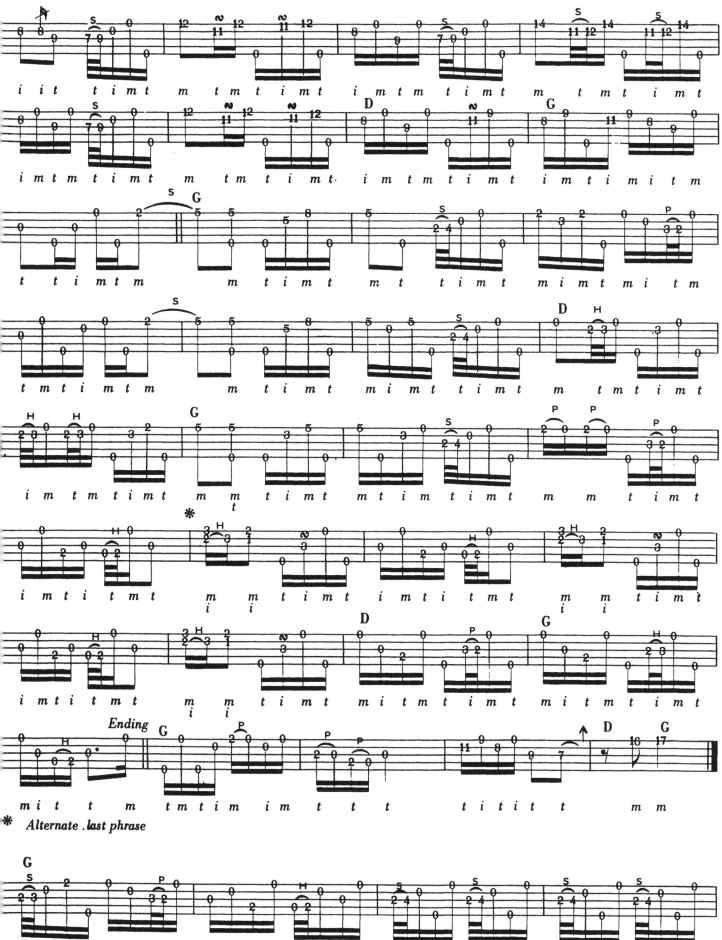

~ Back-up patterns need not be flashy or complicated ~

Try this simple back-up "vamping" or "boom-chick" style pattern
to John Henry with the suggested different chord positions.

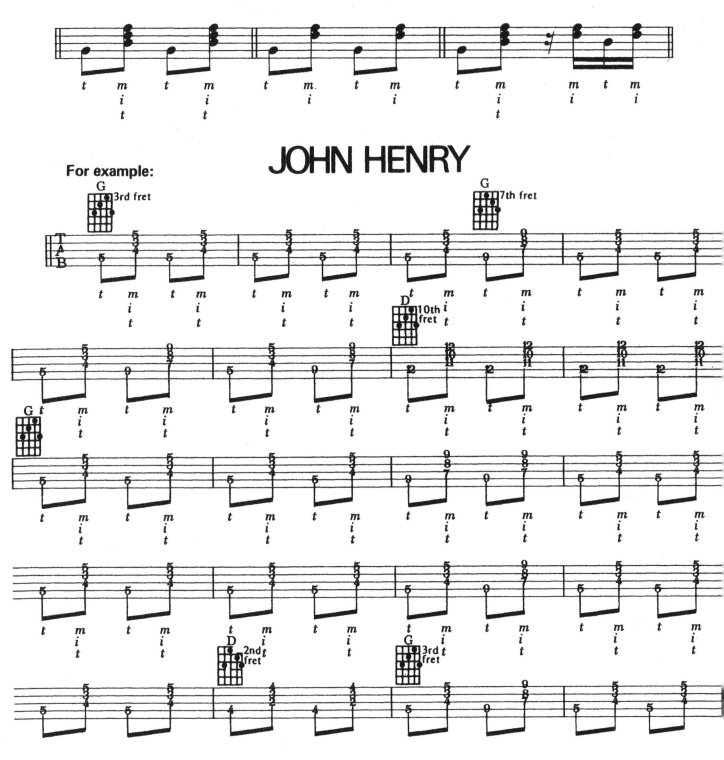

JOHN HENRY

Below are a few different roll patterns,
While playing the "boom-chick' pattern try putting in a few of these roll patterns.

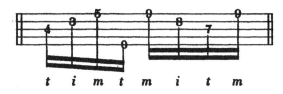

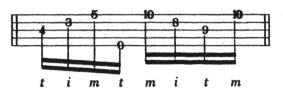

Little Maggie

Traditional

Arranged by:
Douglas Dillard

1. Oh, well yon - der stands lit - tle Mag - gie with a dram glass in her hand. She's a - drink - ing a - way her trou - bles she's a court - in' an - oth - er man.

2. Sometimes I have a nickel,
sometimes I have a dime.
Someday I'll have ten dollars,
I'll pay little Maggie's fine.

3. Pretty flowers were made for bloomin',
pretty stars were made to shine.
Pretty women were made for lovin',
little Maggie was made to be mine.

4. Lay down your last cold dollar,
lay down your gold watch and chain.
Little Maggie's gonna dance for daddy,
listen to this old banjer ring.

5. Go away, go away little Maggie,
go and do the best you can.
I'll get me another women,
you can get you another man.

Little Maggie

Arranged by:
Douglas Dillard

Traditional

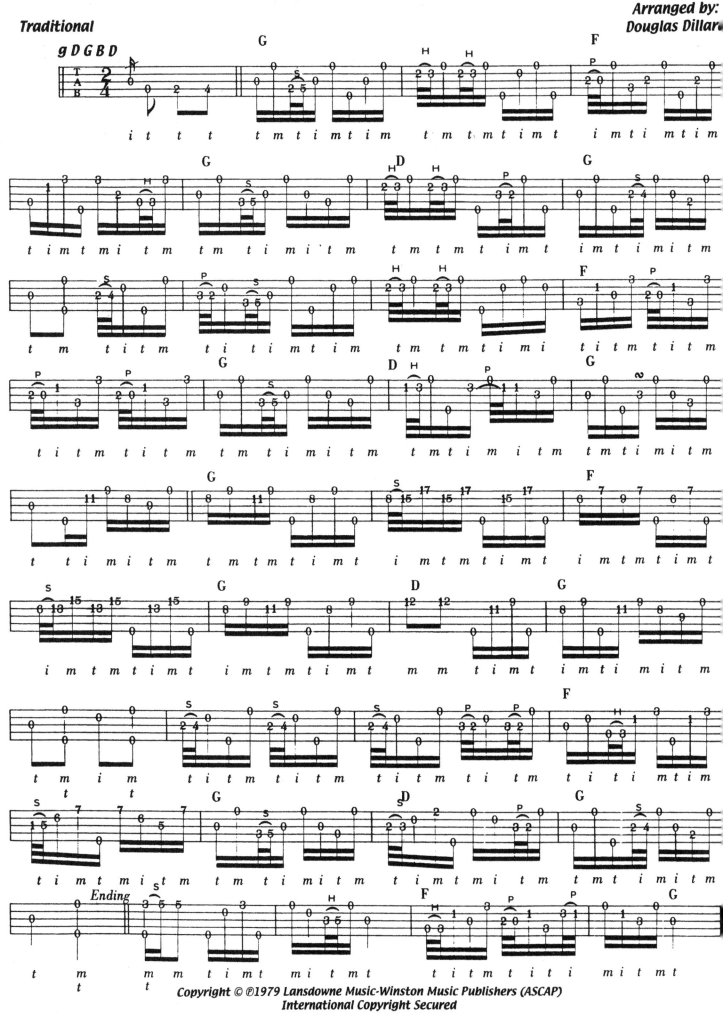

Chord Rhythm Pattern

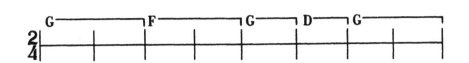

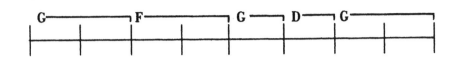

Suggested Back-up Pattern

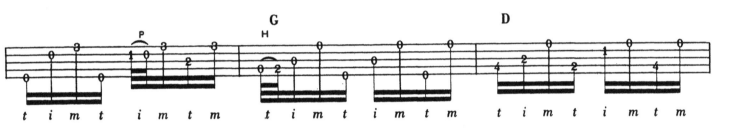

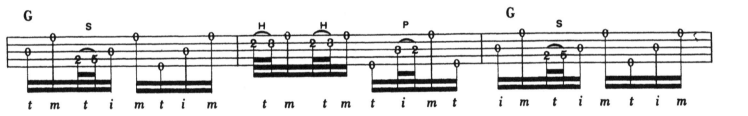

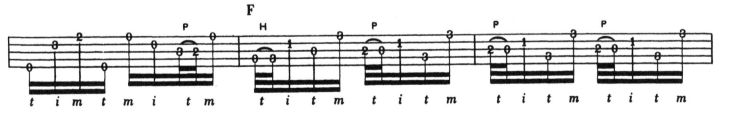

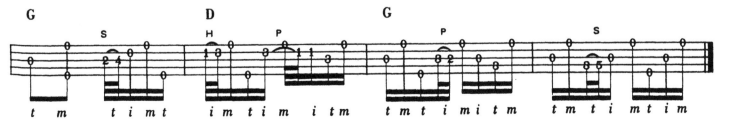

Lonesome Indian

Traditional

Arranged by: Rodney Dillard , Douglas Dillar
Mitch Jayne & Dean Webb

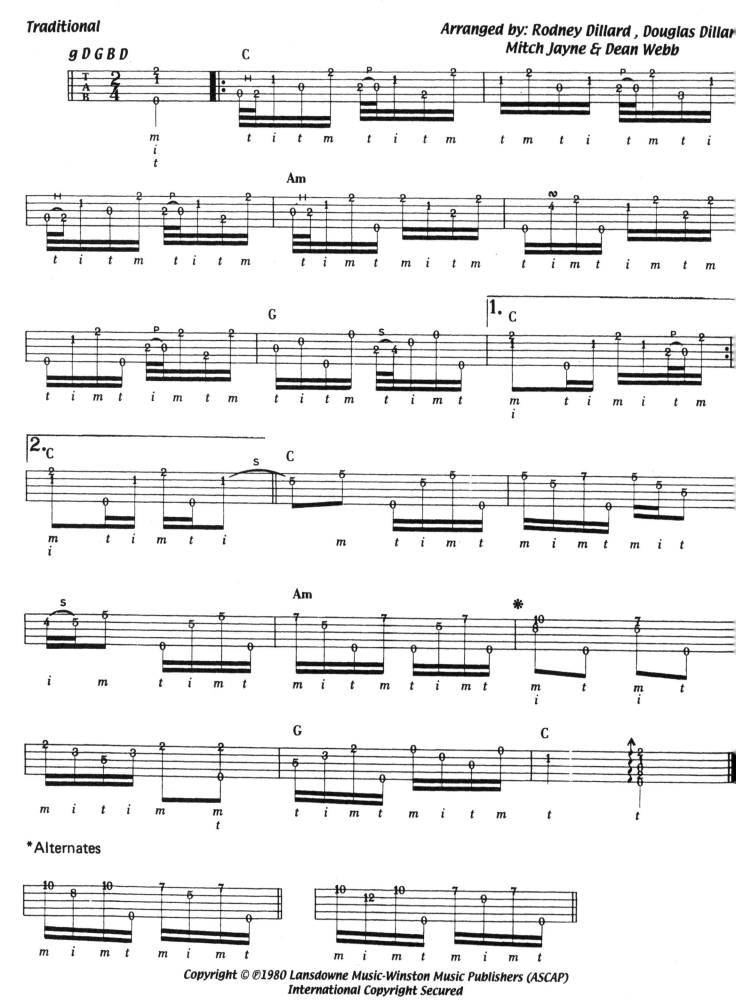

*Alternates

48

Sinkin' Creek

Arranged by: Douglas Dillard

Alternate for first two bars:

Ending:

49

Old Joe Clark

Traditional

Arrangement by:
Douglas Dillard

1. Old Joe Clark, the preach - er's son, preached all o - ver the plain. The on - ly text he ev - er knew was "High, low, Jack and the game."

Chorus: Fare ye well, Old Joe Clark, fare ye well I'm bound. Fare ye well, Old Joe Clark, good - bye Bet - sy Brown.

2. He puts his banjo in my hands
and tells me what to play.
Dances with my pretty little girl
until the break of day.　　　*Chorus*

3. Old Joe Clark had a mule,
his name was Morgan Brown.
And every tooth in that mule's head
was sixteen inches round.　　　*Chorus*

Old Joe Clark

Traditional

**Arrangement by:
Douglas Dillard**

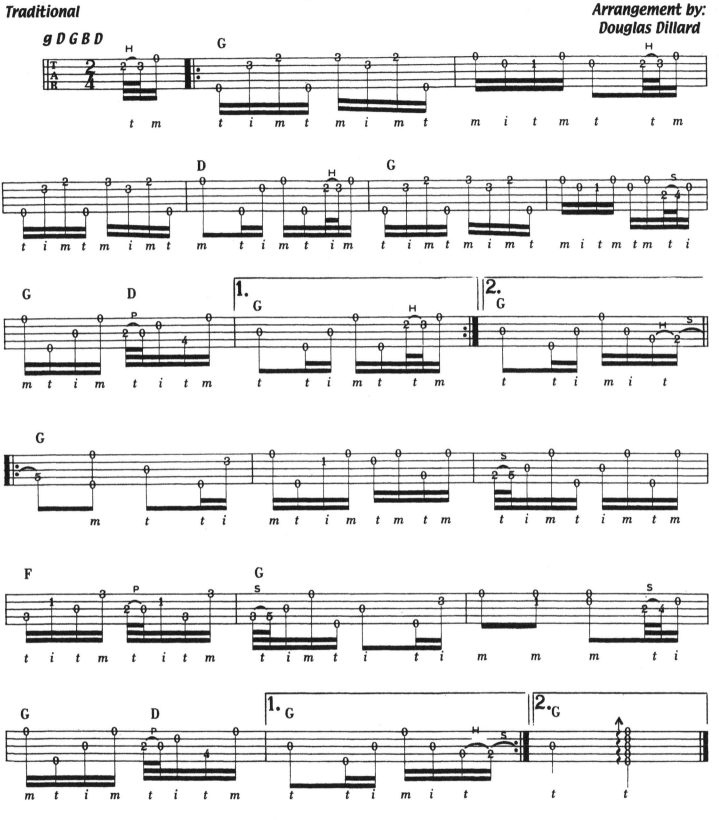

Alternate fingering for second bar, which avoids
having to play the same string twice in a row.

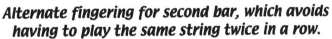

Old Home Place

Words by: Mitch Jayne
Music by: Dean Webb

1. It's been ten long years since I left my home in the hollow where I was born. Where the cool fall nights make the wood smoke rise and a fox hunter blew his horn. What have they done to the old home place; why did they tear it down? And why did I leave the plow in the field and look for a job in the town?

2. I fell in love with a girl in the town,
   I thought that she would be true.
   I ran away to Charlottesville,
   and worked in a sawmill crew.

3. Well, the girl ran off with somebody else;
   the taverns took all my pay
   And here I stand where the old home stood
   before they took it away.

4. Now the geese fly south and the cold wind moans
   as I stand here and hang my head.
   I've lost my love, I've lost my home
   and now I wish that I was dead.

Old Home Place

Arranged by: Douglas Dillard
Words by: Mitch Jayne
Music by: Dean Webb

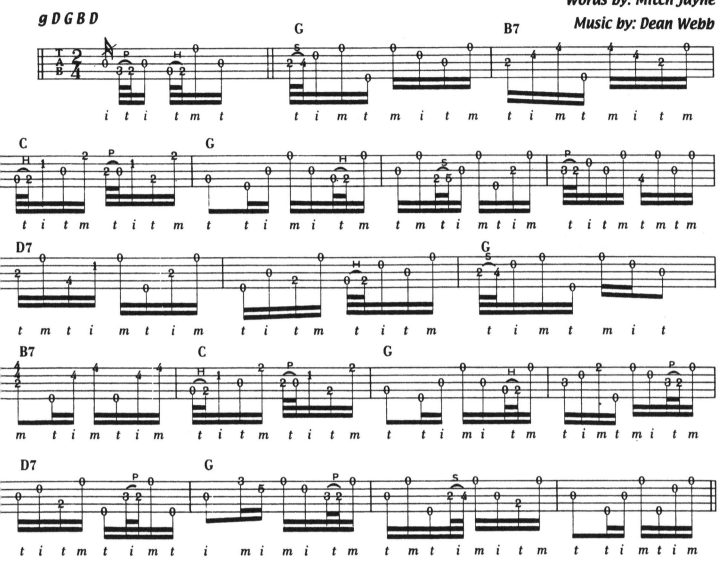

This song was recorded on the Dillards "Back Porch Bluegrass" album. Doug began the song with the first half of this break and Doug Webb played a mandolin solo during the second half. For this arrangement Doug made up the second half.

Just before repeating the chorus for the last time, Dean and Doug took another instrumental break. Doug went second this time and the tab below is what he played.

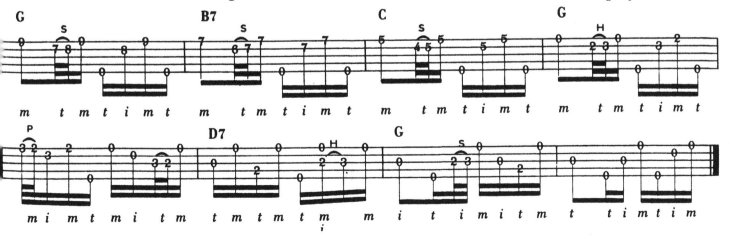

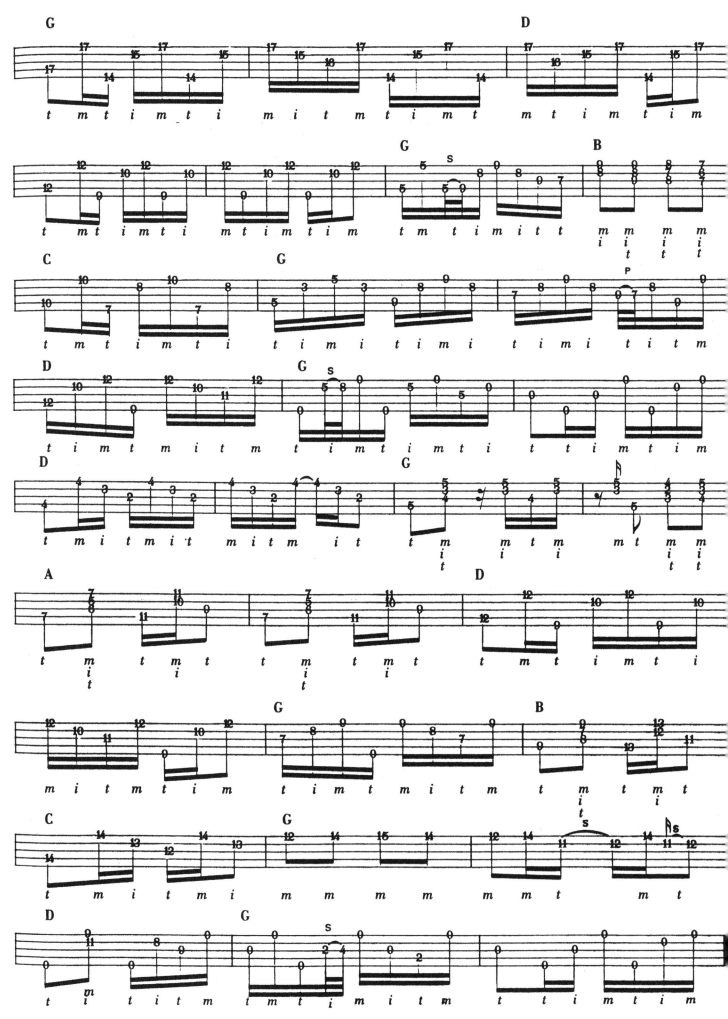

54

Chord Rhythm Pattern

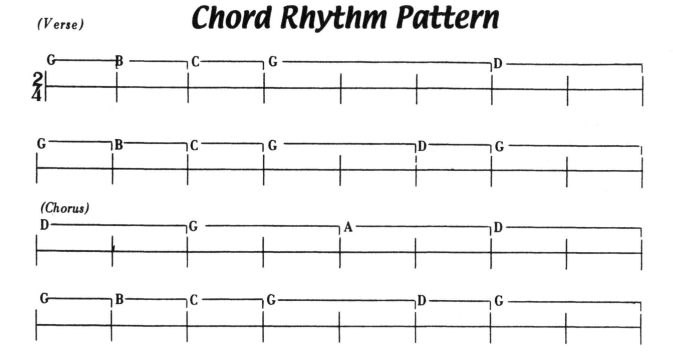

Suggested Back-up Pattern

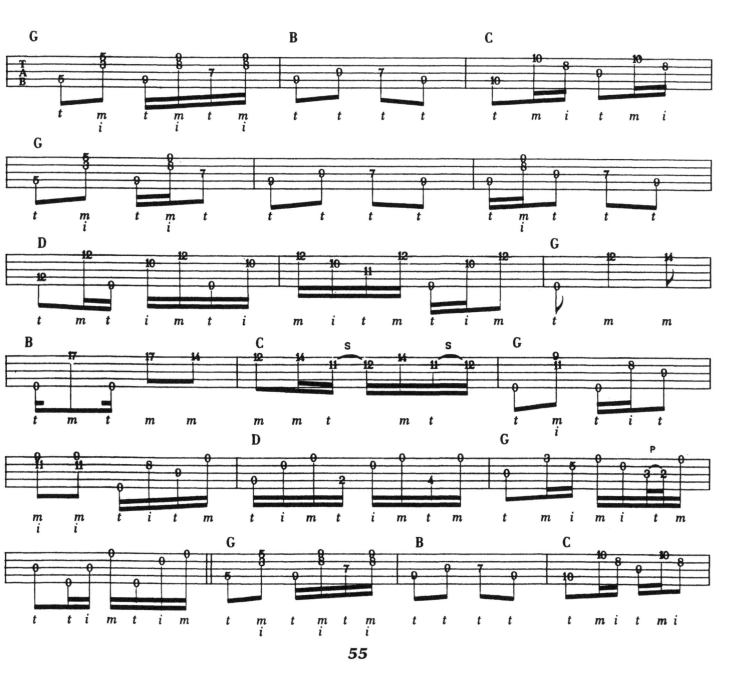

What's That

Music by:
Douglas Dillard

What's That

Capo 2nd fret

Music by:
Douglas Dillard

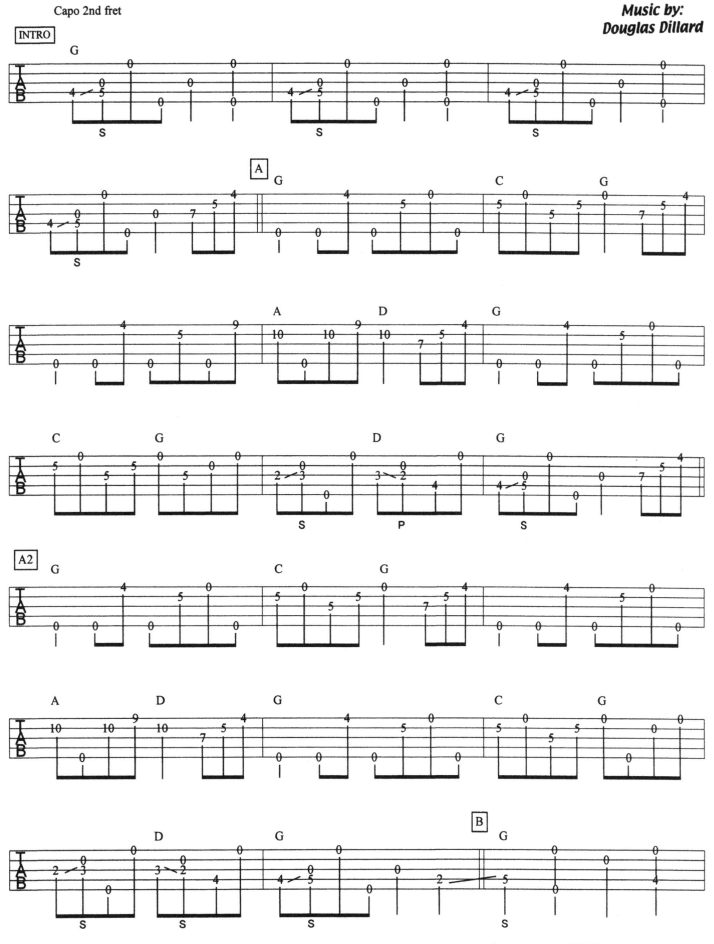

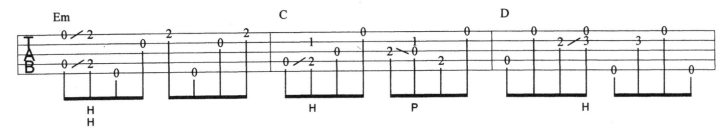

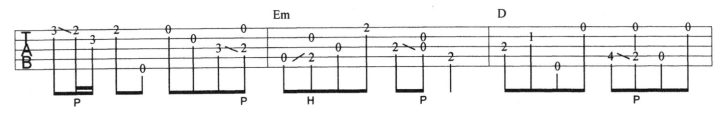

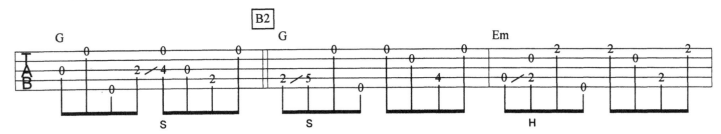

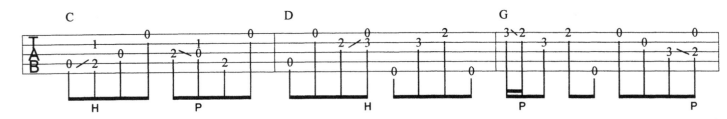

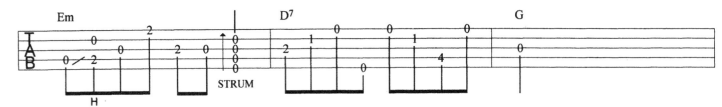

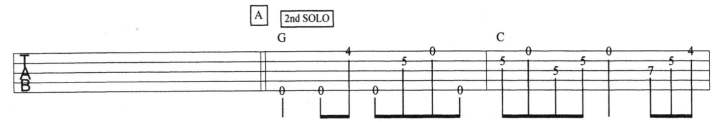

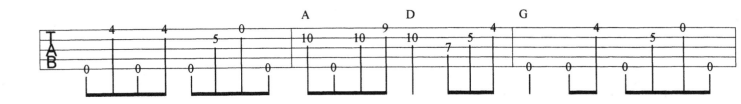

58

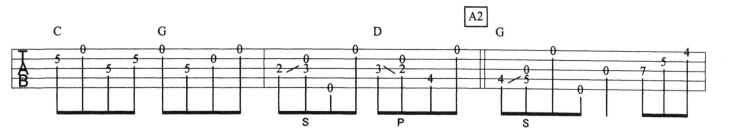

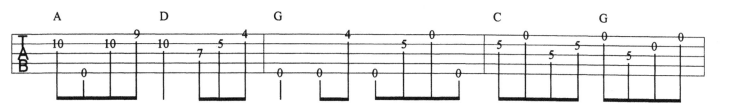

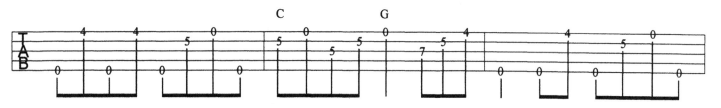

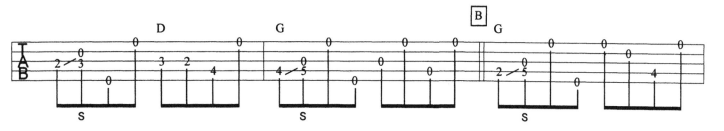

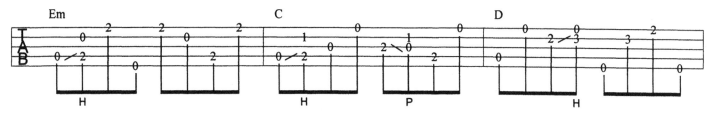

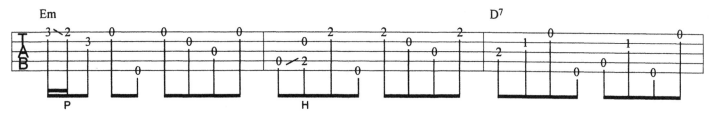

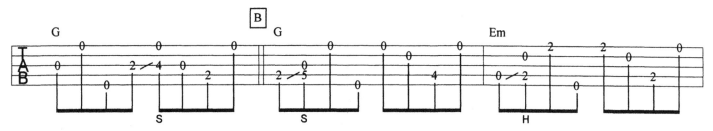

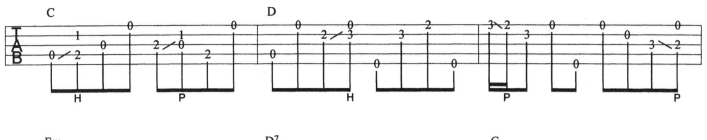

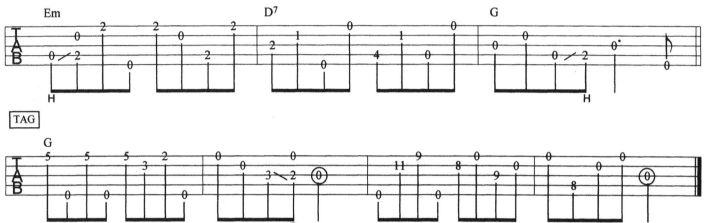

TAG

Buckin' Mule

Traditional

Arrangement by:
Rodney Dillard, Douglas Dillard
Mitch Jayne & Dean Webb

1. Grand-ma had a mu-ley cow, mu-ley when she's born; It took a jay-bird for-ty years to fly from horn to horn. "Whoa, mule whoa, whoa, mule" I say, I ain't got time to kiss you now, the mule has run a-way.

2. Now grandma had a yeller hen,
   yeller as gold.
   She set her on three buzzard eggs
   and hatched-out one old crow.

3. Take this seat Miss Liza,
   just you keep cool.
   I ain't got time to kiss you now,
   I'm foolin' this mule.

4. If I chewed tobacco,
   I tell you what I would do:
   I'd chew it nice and juicy
   and spit it all on you.

5. I'd never marry an old man,
   I'll tell you the reason why:
   his lips all all tobaccer juice,
   he never zips his fly.

Buckin' Mule

*Pick behind the bridge

Chord Rhythm Pattern

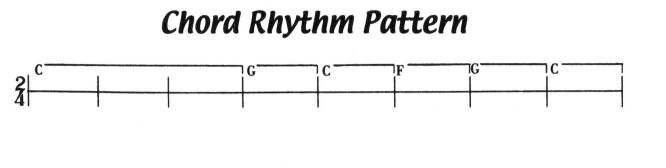

Suggested Back-up Pattern

Andy Griffith and Doug Dillard
on the set of the Andy Griffith TV show

Green Corn

Traditional

Arranged by:
Douglas Dillard

2. All I want in this creation,
   pretty little wife and a big plantation . (play twice)

3. All I need to make me happy,
   two little kids to call me pappy. (play twice)

4. One named Bill, the other named Davy,
   They like their biscuits sopped in gravy. (play twice)

Green Corn

Traditional

In the "two finger" style. This was the first tune Doug ever learned.

Arranged by:
Douglas Dillard

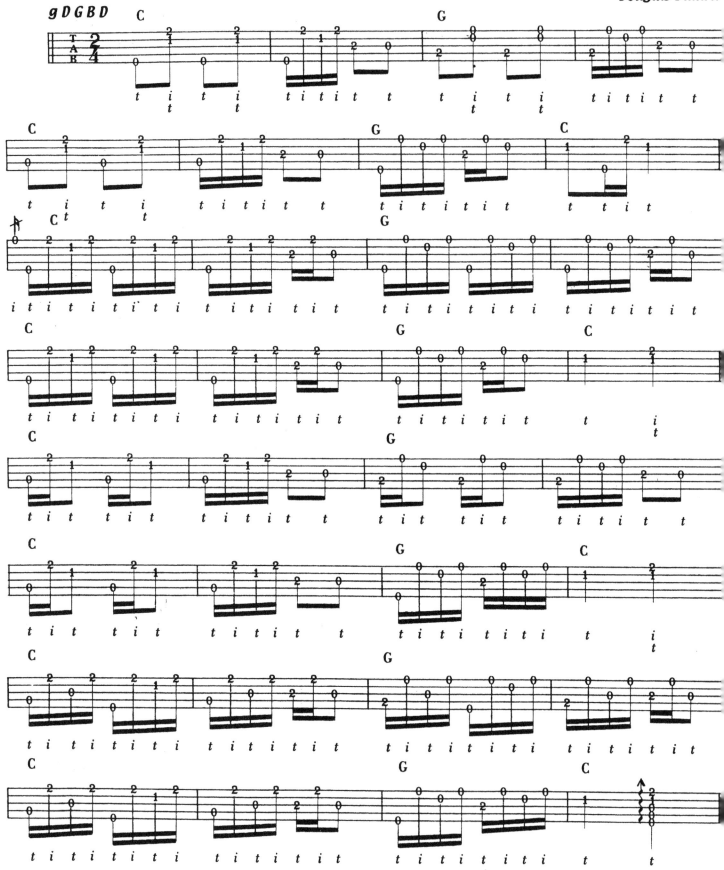

Whole World Round

Words by: Mitch Jayne
Music by: Joe Stuart
Arranged by: Douglas Dillard

1. I heard my neigh-bor's roos-ter crow ___ ear-ly in the day; I heard his ax be-yond the hill ___ and now I'm bound ___ a-way. 2. For some men love the cit-y life, ___ some men crave the town, but I'll be bound for the lone-some woods ___ where I can set-tle down. Fid-dle and a bow and a fire-light's glow, you can hear that lone-some

D. C. (3rd & 4th Verse)

sound. I'll leave be-hind my trou-bl-in' mind and go the whole world round.

3. **The red squirrel leaves when the grey squirrel comes,**
   the eagles nest alone;
   A hundred miles from a wagon track
   is where I'll build my home.

4. **I see the old man whittlin' wood,**
   I see the streets of town.
   I packed my goods for the Arkansas woods,
   and there I'll settle down.

Whole World Round

Arranged by: Douglas Dilla
Words by: Mitch Jayne
Music by: Joe Stuart

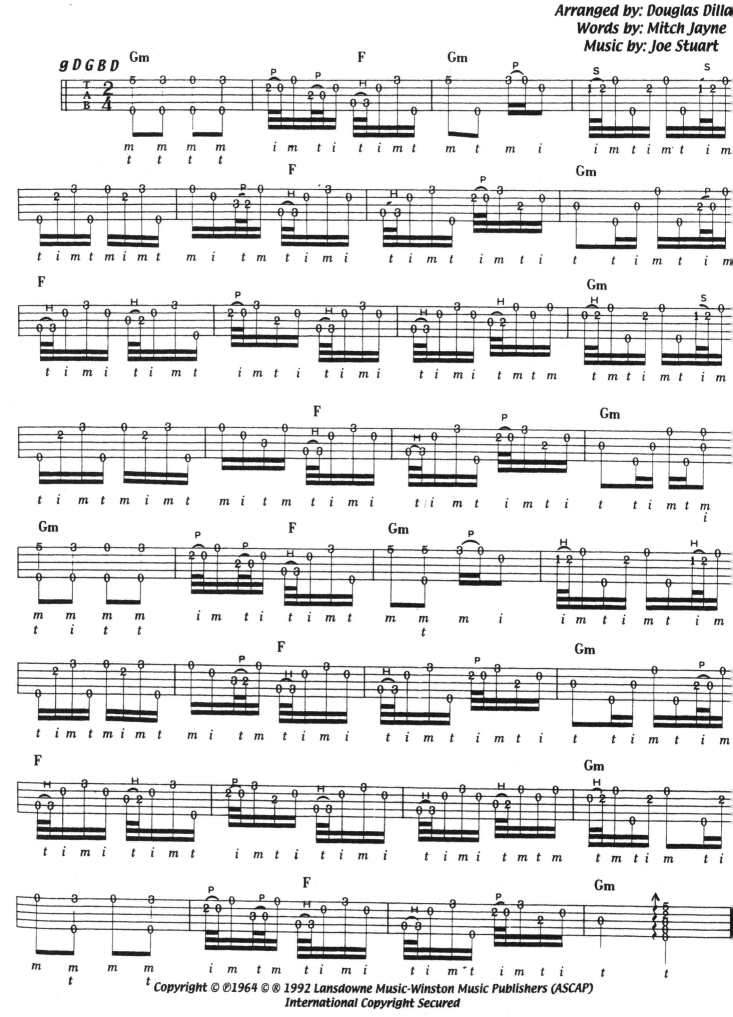

Discography of Douglas Dillard

Featuring his solo recordings and with Gene Clark, The Dillards, The Doug Dillard Band and on Compilations.

Dillard & Clark - Through the Morning through the Night (A&M)
Gene Clark & Douglas Dillard (A&M-dutch)
Dillard and Clark - the Fantastic Expedition of (A&M)
Grass Roots - Dillard & Clark & The Flying Burrito Brothers (A&M)
Kansas City Southern - Doug Dillard & Gene Clark (Ariola-Eurodisc)
There is a Time - Anthology - The Dillards (Vanguard)
Country Tracks - Best of the Dillards (Elektra - Warner Pioneer)
Back Porch Bluegrass - The Dillards (Elektra)
Pickin and Fiddlin - The Dillards with Byron Berline (Elektra)
The Banjo Album (Sierra)
The Dillards - Decade Waltz (Flying Fish)
Heaven - Douglas Dillard (Flying Fish)
Homecoming & Family Reunion (Flying Fish)
Dillard - Hartford - Dillard - Permanent Wave (Flying Fish)
Dillard - Hartford - Dillard (Flying Fish)
The First Time Live - The Dillards (Varese/Vintage)
The Dillards - Live Almost (Elektra)
Douglas Flint Dillard (20th Century)
Jackrabbit - Doug Dillard (Flying Fish)
Duelin Banjo - Doug Dillard (20th Century)
Heartbreak Hotel - The Doug Dillard Band (Flying Fish)
What's That - The Doug Dillard Band (Flying Fish)
Bluegrass Breakdown - Newport Folk Festival (Vanguard)
Generations of Bluegrass - compilation Vol. 3 (Vanguard)
Shoulder to Shoulder Vol. 2 compilation (Vanguard)
Bluegrass Essentials Vol. 1 compilation (UNI/Hip-O)
Appalacian Stomp - Bluegrass Classics - compilation (Rhino/Wea)
Greatest Stars of Folk Music - compilation (Legacy/DNA)

*does not include singles.

Douglas Dillard's Music an also be heard in the film score of Vanishing Point, and in Bunny O'Hare as well as in TV Show's - The Andy Griffith Show, Return to Mayberry and Monty Python.

More Great Banjo Books from Centerstream...

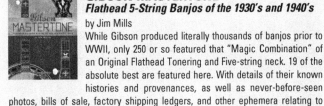